T0000712

The Media and Me

A Guide to Critical Media Literacy

FOR YOUNG PEOPLE

The Media and Me

A Guide to Critical Media Literacy

FOR YOUNG PEOPLE

PROJECT CENSORED AND THE MEDIA REVOLUTION COLLECTIVE

ILLUSTRATIONS BY PETER GLANTING

TRIANGLE SQUARE
books for young readers

CP
THE CENSORED
— PRESS —

NEW YORK ■ FAIR OAKS, CA

A JOINT PRODUCTION OF THE CENSORED PRESS AND
TRIANGLE SQUARE BOOKS FOR YOUNG READERS

Copyright © 2022 by The Censored Press and the Media Revolution Collective

All rights reserved. No part of this book may be reproduced, stored in a retrieval system, or transmitted in any form or by any means, including mechanical, electronic, photocopying, recording, or otherwise, without the prior written permission of the publisher.

Seven Stories Press   The Censored Press
140 Watts Street   P.O. Box 1177
New York, NY 10013   Fair Oaks, CA 95628
sevenstories.com   censoredpress.org

College professors and high school and middle school teachers may order free examination copies of Seven Stories Press titles. Visit https://www.sevenstories.com/pg/resources-academics or email academics@sevenstories.com.

Library of Congress Cataloging-in-Publication Data

Names: Project Censored (U.S.), author.
Title: The media and me : a guide to critical media literacy for young
    people / by Project Censored and the Media Revolution Collective.
Identifiers: LCCN 2022022384 | ISBN 9781644211960 (trade paperback) | ISBN
    9781644211946 (hardcover) | ISBN 9781644211953 (ebook)
Subjects: LCSH: Media literacy--Juvenile literature. | Mass
    media--Objectivity--Juvenile literature.
Classification: LCC P96.M4 P75 2022 | DDC 302.23--dc23/eng/20220525
LC record available at https://lccn.loc.gov/2022022384

Printed in the USA.

9 8 7 6 5 4 3 2

DEDICATION

In loving memory of the students, teachers, and staff
whose lives have been cut short by gun violence
in schools across the United States.
Classrooms should be places of learning, not violence.

Contents

CALL-OUT BOXES
(IN-CHAPTER ACTIVITIES)

Looking Beneath the Surface

We use clocks to know what time it is. Between the invention of hourglasses and digital clocks, there were analog watches—watches with hands and faces—which were the main devices we used to measure time.

Along with learning the ABCs and how to ride a bike, you probably learned to tell time using an old-fashioned clock. You might not have thought much about learning to tell time since then. It's easy to take a skill for granted once you've mastered it. It becomes second nature, which is good because that allows you to focus attention on other things. Instead of  thinking, "I can tell time!," you look at a clock and think, "Only fifteen minutes until I am out of this class!"

Back then, you had to learn how to interpret the clock's two "arms"—the little arm that measures hours, the big arm that measures minutes—in relation to the numbers, from one to twelve, on the clock's circular background. You had to learn, for example, that when the big hand was on the twelve and the little hand was on the three, it was three o'clock. Learning to tell time was all about understanding the relationship between the clock's hands and numbers. Once you understood that, you knew how to tell time.

In your lifetime, you've probably seen these types of clockfaces on wall clocks and on wristwatches. You've also witnessed how digital technologies have made it easier to tell time. Instead of having to make sense of the hands on the clock, we just read the numbers from digital displays on our smartphones, or on our computers, or in our cars. You may even be able to call on digital assistants such as Alexa or Siri to tell you what time it is.

But what if the clock breaks and you want to fix it? Or what if you are just curious to know more about why the clock works the way it does? Then you need to know more than how to tell time; you need to learn how to look beneath the surface of the clock's face, to observe and understand the mechanisms that drive the motion of the clock's hands.

Telling time is one thing; understanding how the clock works is something else.

Wait a minute here, you may be thinking, I thought this was a book about media literacy (whatever that might be . . .). What's all this about clocks and learning to tell time? Put another way: What can a clock teach us about media and media literacy?

You do not need to understand how a video is produced to enjoy YouTube, or how news is reported to read the *New York Times*, or how algorithms work in order to post content on Facebook, Instagram, or TikTok. Each of those activities is sort of like telling time: you can do them without much background knowledge. But if you want to understand why and how YouTube, the *New York Times*, or your favorite social media platform highlights some people, topics, and ideas while rendering others all but invisible, you need to know more. You need to look beneath the surface to understand the hidden but real mechanisms that shape media content and influence how we interpret it.

Critical Media Literacy

What interests us, the authors of this book, is a concept known as *critical media literacy*. Critical media literacy (or CML, for short) addresses these typically concealed, but always powerful, inner workings. Critical media literacy gets into the hidden mechanics that drive our mass media of news, information, and entertainment. CML education is a way to learn about the world, especially the world of media. According to statistical research, people around your

age spend more than eleven hours a day with some form of media—and usually, you are **media multitasking**—that is, using more than one tool or technology at once.[1]

Given that you spend so much time with so much media, we believe you deserve to have a robust understanding of how that media works. That's why we think this form of knowing is especially important today.

Critical media literacy is about asking questions more than it is about learning the right answers. Through CML, we not only explore *what* we know but also ask *how* we know it. We explore what we like, what we believe, and why. When practicing CML, we employ a collection of skills that help us move from being passive consumers of media to becoming engaged critics and creators.

Meaning, Access and Representation, and Validity

Throughout *The Media and Me*, we will develop the themes of *meaning, access and representation*, and *validity*. These ideas are so important to understanding the media that we want to introduce them here. Reflecting back on the clock metaphor that opened this chapter, meaning, access and representation, and validity represent the inner workings, or gears, of media literacy. Examining them will help us understand how and why media institutions operate the way they do.

Meaning is the most slippery of the terms because it is so fundamental to everything we do. In an influential article from 1973, the anthropologist Clifford Geertz used the examples of blinking and winking to get at the idea of meaning. Both actions involve what we might describe as "rapid movement of the eyelid over the eye," but you do not need to be some famous social scientist to know that winks are different from blinks. If you get a speck of dust in your eye and your eye twitches, you do not necessarily attach any meaning to that action. You're just blinking. But when you wink at your friend, that same eyelid movement could mean anything from "just kidding" to "I am flirting." Being able to tell blinks from winks depends on making sense of what we know and how we know it. And if that wink is going to work, all of this interpretation has to happen very quickly.

We attach meaning to actions, so gestures and body language allow us to communicate without words. But this does not mean that everyone always agrees about what something means. Because meaning is subject to interpretation, and our perspectives can vary, people sometimes have different interpretations about what something means. Think of the color red. In some contexts red is associated with passion, or love; in other situations red might convey heat; and when someone says they're seeing red, that can mean they're angry. The basic point is that meaning depends on interpretation, and interpretations can vary from person to person and from group to group depending on context.

Asking questions about meaning is one way to begin developing a critical stance regarding media. How do you make sense of the imagery in your favorite TV show or video game or YouTube video? What is its message? Of course, meaning is conveyed through language too. So whether we're talking about a poem or a news story, we can ask how an author's choice of words conveys meaning, and how different readers might interpret the author's word choice in significantly different ways. Because critical media literacy depends on interpretation, meaning is a concept we'll come back to again and again.

Access and representation are also basic concepts for understanding media more fully. **Access** opens up questions about who is included and who is excluded. As we'll discuss in later chapters, access can be as simple as whether or not you have a computer with an internet connection. **Representation** can have two meanings. (Hey, there's that concept of meaning coming up again already!) First,

representation can refer to the way that images and texts reconstruct, rather than reflect, the original sources that they represent.

For anyone interested in media, this type of representation is very important. A photograph—whether it's a social media post about a tropical vacation or a news photograph of a public demonstration—is not equivalent to the sensory experience of the sun, the sand, and the breaking waves on that beach, or what it feels like to march alongside dozens of other people down the middle of a public street where police with batons block the way forward. Asking about representation reminds us, "The map is not the territory."

Representation has a second important meaning for people interested in media. We can ask questions such as "Who is represented?" and "How are they represented?" Examining representation in this sense encourages us to think not only about individuals but also about groups and categories of people. In this usage, representation alerts us to issues of difference and, potentially, inequality. For example, how often do news stories actually include people who are poor—not just as the invisible subjects of reports about poverty, but as actual living people who have ideas, concerns, and aspirations of their own? Questions like this link representation and access: a concern for access can lead us to look beneath the surface of media content, by asking who is included and put at the center of stories, and who is excluded or marginalized. Chapter 4 will investigate representation in more detail to examine how our identities are both shaped by and shown in the media.

Validity is the quality of being legitimate or genuine. If you say that some claim is valid, that means you have reason to believe it is true. The emphasis here should be on the phrase "reason to believe." A claim is not valid because you say it is so; instead, it is valid because you can provide evidence to justify it—and you can defend the claim even in the face of counter-evidence.

Think of validity as a kind of solid footing. When we adopt a critical stance toward media, we ask questions about meaning—and meaning, as we have seen, is open to multiple interpretations, including competing interpretations. This situation might be enough to make you throw up your hands in despair and say, "Who cares? It's all just a matter of opinion in the end." This is when validity, and a host of principles that can help give us confidence that a statement or story is true, come to the rescue. Some differences of interpretation *are* a matter of opinion. But many differences in interpretation can be resolved by considering the evidence for and against each of the competing interpretations. For example, you and a friend may disagree about how *good* a musician is. Your disagreement may be solved by saying it is a difference of opinion. However, you may be able to point to the singer's musical training, or how many top hits they've had, to illustrate that they have a certain level of ability that deserves consideration. Asking questions about validity helps to distinguish facts from opinions. Validity is also a core idea in critical thinking, a topic that we take up in more detail in chapter 2.

How Media Literate Are You?

In 2016, the Stanford History Education Group (SHEG), a group of researchers from Stanford University, released the findings of their two-year study of how well young people evaluate and interpret information found on the internet.[2] Based on the findings of the SHEG research, young people are *not* media literate. The study's participants included students from middle school through college, all of whom had trouble telling the difference between news and advertisements, recognizing point of view or bias, and identifying who owns or runs certain websites. What the SHEG researchers determined was that young people spend a great deal of *time* with media but do not know how it works. Young people are adept at *making use* of media, but not necessarily great at evaluating it. Young people make active decisions about their media of choice, but some do not know much beyond what they see on the screen. The researchers found that many young people do not know how to analyze what is "behind the scenes," including what many scholars call the "means of production." Drawing from our opening narrative, we might say that the SHEG researchers found that a lot of young people know how to tell time—but they do not know how the clock works.

Do not be discouraged by this! This book will help you be part of a shift away from the dilemma that this research describes! And it's not your fault. Do adults do much better? We all have a responsibility to teach ourselves and each other CML. In the pages that follow, you will help flip the script and develop an enhanced understanding of media literacy.

Inside *The Media and Me*

Hopefully by now you are fired up and ready to dive in. We are *not* interested in making you turn off the media that you use, or denying you the pleasure and joy that the media can provide. We like media too! What we want is to provide you with some ways to be a critically media-literate citizen rather than merely a consumer of media. A **critically media-literate citizen** is a person who accesses, analyzes, evaluates, creates, and acts with media to empower themselves and others.

That term—"critically media-literate citizen"—is an important one, but it's also a mouthful. From here on, we'll simply say **media citizen**; what we mean is a person who engages their critical media literacy skills when they use media.

Media citizens reflect on how

they are using media. Most importantly, media citizens think critically about the media they use. To be critical does not mean to dislike. We can be critical of something *and* find great joy in it simultaneously.

In fact, sometimes thinking critically about something increases our enjoyment of it! To be critical is to take a step back from the media content we consume in order to examine it more thoroughly. This book will help you begin to look beneath the surface and challenge media narratives.

Chapters 1 and 2 examine in more detail the foundations of critical media literacy, including a close examination of how the media industries are organized and the elements of critical thinking. Chapter 3 distinguishes *critical* media literacy from other types of media literacy. Critical media literacy focuses on the role of power in shaping the production, distribution, and interpretation of media. Chapter 4 focuses on representation in the media, with attention to the puzzle pieces that make up our identity, including our race and ethnicity, gender, sexuality, language and accent and dialect, ability, economic class, and family structure. Chapter 5 puts the emphasis on critical media *literacy*. If the term "literacy" typically refers to the ability to read and write, then what does media literacy involve? Chapter 6 focuses on the pervasive influence of advertising and the taken-for-granted culture of consumption. Chapter 7 directs attention to news and journalism. This chapter encourages a deeper look at the popular topic of news "bias" by showing how economic interests, political interests, and journalists' reliance on official sources all impact the construction of news stories. The last chapter of *The Media and Me* is about putting what you've learned from the book's previous chapters into action. We do not just want you to *read* this book; we hope that reading it will inspire you to *get involved*. Finally, *The Media and Me* ends with a glossary of key terms and concepts and suggested readings, if you want to investigate further the ideas presented in this book.

Critical thinking means asking questions that encourage us to rethink assumptions we might otherwise have, and searching for evidence to support the positions we hold. We will address how to ask purposeful questions, build sound arguments, recognize fallacies or mistakes in reasoning, determine what constitutes evidence, and raise awareness about the many biases that can invisibly but significantly shape our perception of the world.

We will examine the role of media in the lifelong process of **socialization**—how we learn values and a way of life from those around us. We will consider how media content, from music videos and movies to social media streams and news broadcasts, are specific forms of one fundamental human activity, storytelling. We examine how media are fundamental not only to the communication of information but also to collaboration among people and the creation of community. We also consider how economic interests shape the media you consume, by looking at the connection between media ownership and media content. We will introduce a powerful framework—known as the *encoding-decoding model of communication*—for examining how media messages are produced, distributed, and interpreted. If you are interested in changing the world for the better, the encoding-decoding model will likely thrill you.

Who We Are and How We Wrote This Book

We are a collection of ten authors, with distinct life stories and professional backgrounds. We include among us college students, high school and college teachers, activists, and scholars of critical media literacy. We've studied sociology, media studies, history, journalism, and education. We are male, female, gender nonbinary, heterosexual, and queer. We are working- to middle-class. We are white, Black, and Brown. We are all able-bodied. Three of us have children. Some of us are cat people, some of us are dog people, and some of us are learning to be dog people while still loving our cats. We are different people with at least one thing in common: we are committed to learning, practicing, and sharing our work in critical media literacy because we think it is vitally important.

In writing this book, we worked to make sure that any claim we made came with evidence. You will see that we have endnotes so that you can follow up on the sources we used in our research. Throughout the book, you will see certain words or phrases that are **bolded**; these are important and useful terms. You can find their definitions in the glossary at the back of the book. Throughout the text you will find "Call-Out Boxes" that give you the opportunity, if you so choose, to take some of the ideas further by doing some media analysis of your own. We envision this book as a bit of a "choose your own adventure": you may choose to read it straight through, beginning with this first chapter, or you may choose to dip in and out of chapters whose topics particularly interest you.

Freedom of Opinion and Expression as Human Rights

In 1948, the General Assembly of the United Nations adopted and proclaimed the Universal Declaration of Human Rights, defining standards to recognize and protect the dignity of all human beings. The Declaration includes a preamble and thirty articles that specify rights that are universal and inalienable. That means people everywhere in the world are entitled to the protections they provide: You cannot voluntarily give them up, nor should anyone else take them away from you.

Article 19 of the Declaration addresses the rights to opinion and expression:

Everyone has the right to freedom of opinion and expression; this right includes freedom to hold opinions without interference and to seek, receive and impart information and ideas through any media and regardless of frontiers.[3]

The notion that it is our universal, inalienable right to "seek, receive and impart information and ideas through any media and regardless of frontiers" is a remarkable, perhaps revolutionary, claim. The idea that this right extends "regardless of frontiers" might sound like something from science fiction. Indeed, back in 1948, when the original members of the United Nations established the Universal Declaration of Human Rights, the technology to seek, receive, and impart information "regardless of frontiers" was pretty limited compared to the power of our contemporary means of communication.

But what inspires us about Article 19 is not how much technology has developed since 1948, although those changes *are* amazing. Instead we conclude this first chapter by introducing freedom of opinion and expression as fundamental human rights because this idea drives all the work that we do.

Think of the ideals expressed in Article 19 as being like the master gear in the clock that we considered at the start of this chapter. The rights to expression and opinion provide the energy and drive for *all* the other mechanisms that make the watch work and allow us to tell time. Freedom of expression and opinion are so fundamental that we cannot even imagine critical media literacy without them. What, after all, is the point of understanding how media work if you cannot use them to form and express opinions of your own?

Of course, just because an organization such as the United Nations asserts that freedom of opinion and expression are universal, inalienable rights does not mean this is automatically true for everyone everywhere. You probably do not need to read any further in this book to think of ways that corporations, governments, or perhaps even people you know actually *interfere* in ways that contradict the ideals expressed in Article 19.

The gap between the ideals expressed in Article 19 of the Universal Declaration of Human Rights and the reality of the world we live in also inspires us to pursue critical media literacy. Critical media literacy gives us a way to assess that gulf *and* to figure out how to bring the actual world a little bit more in alignment with the lofty vision of a world in which *everyone* is free "to seek, receive and impart information and ideas through any media and regardless of frontiers."

CHAPTER I

What Are Media?

Mobile Screens and "Looking Glass" Selves

Your sense of self—who you are, what you like, how you interpret the world—has developed through relationships with other people. Through a lifelong process that begins with family and extends to include friends and teachers, and will increasingly also include the people you work with, you're learning a way of life and how to make it your own.

Charles Cooley, an early twentieth-century sociologist from Chicago, coined the term "looking-glass self" to suggest how this process of **socialization** works.[4] Using the metaphor of reflecting mirrors, Cooley proposed that the self develops through our perception of others' evaluations and appraisals of us. We see ourselves as we think others see us. If you believe other people see you as "cool" or "athletic" or "funny," then that shapes how you think and feel about yourself.

Cooley developed the idea of our looking-glass selves

long before the invention of smartphones, social media, or even the first television broadcast in the United States. (That happened in 1928.) His idea that our sense of self is *reflected* makes even more sense in an era where mobile phone screens, computer screens, and television screens are omnipresent.

Critically media-literate citizens recognize that in the twenty-first century, the media shape our looking-glass selves as much as family, friends, and teachers do. We may not feel as though we have relationships with our smartphones, computers, or televisions, but through  these devices we do form relationships and values that exert strong (but often unrecognized) influences on what interests or bores us, who we admire or loathe, and what we wish for or fear. If the media you engage with play important roles in shaping your sense of self and identity, then the question "What are media?" becomes one interesting way to develop a deeper understanding of yourself and your place in the world.

What Are Media?

As a word, "media" is the plural of "medium." A **medium** is a channel of information; **media** are multiple channels of information. Some media scholars define the media of communication as "the different technological processes that facilitate communication between . . . the sender of a message and the receiver of that message."[5] Others distinguish between "media"—the various channels of communication—and "the media," meaning the powerful institutions that control those channels and access to them.[6] You are growing up in a media-saturated world—that is, a world where you are surrounded by digital and analog tools that receive and transmit information. Young people spend up to eleven hours per day engaging with various media, often using different forms of media simultaneously. Caught in the relentless surge of media messages that shape our "looking glass" selves, we want to avoid being snared by superficial appearances or tricked by distorted reflections. A deeper understanding of media helps us navigate these currents without losing our way.

While newspapers, magazines, and books have been around since the seventeenth century, and radio and film were invented in the nineteenth century, the look and production of media that we find most familiar today started in the twentieth century. Television, electronic or battery-powered music listening devices (including record players, cassette decks, and CD players), computers, and the internet were all invented in the twentieth century.

While there are a host of new media in the twenty-first century—especially social media, streaming services, and smartphones—much of what we *do* with those media draw on the "old-fashioned" skills of traditional literacy. For example, when we access a news story via an Instagram feed, that is definitely different from a printed newspaper arriving on our front stoop. Nevertheless, we employ the same literacy skills of our grandparents and great-grandparents. When we watch a movie, whether through a streaming service, on our smartphone, or while on an airplane, we are doing the same thing that people in the mid-twentieth century did when they got dressed up to go to a movie theater, bought a ticket with an assigned seat, and were brought to that seat by an usher. Today's media technologies and how we access them are wildly different from the technologies and access of generations past—yet we can employ some foundational skills to better understand how our technologies have changed over time to become what they are now, and to help us understand how they may change in the future. What you are doing with your media is radically different from what was done in the past *and yet* your media use employs many of the same skills fostered and refined through generations of media use. By extension, how you and your peers use media today can have impacts on how media evolve in the future. The media of today have been shaped by previous peoples' use of media; the media of the future will be influenced by the kinds of choices you and your peers make.

How Much Time Do You Spend with Media? How Much Time Can You Go without It?

How much time do you spend with the media? How "invisible" is the media in your world because so much of it seems available at all times?

You can do a little self-experiment to get a better idea of how much media you use, and for what purpose. For twenty-four hours, keep note of all the media you use. Take some time to reflect on this use: What do you use the most? Is it the media you get the most enjoyment from? How do you feel when you are using it? What have you learned about your media habits?

Now, just out of curiosity, see how long you can go with no media. This might be more challenging than you imagine! How long did you last? What did you learn from those seconds, minutes, hours, or days?

As channels of information, the media teach us a lot; but the media are also socializing agents. As we grow up, we learn about the world through our families, our communities, our schools, maybe our faith. We also learn about the world through the media, especially through **representation** (what the media show) and *lack* of representation (what the media do not show).

Media and Storytelling

Telling stories is among the oldest human activities. You could even argue that storytelling is what makes us human. Whether seated around a campfire under the starry night sky or on a cafeteria bench during school lunch, from ancient times to the present, humans have gathered together to share stories. Not all stories are shared verbally, face to face, or through word of mouth. From cave art made more than 30,000 years ago to the most recent update of your social  media feed, humans have used imagery and language in a variety of media, not only to entertain but also to convey information and transmit lessons: stories help us remember the past and imagine the future (either a better one or a dystopian alternative); stories help us understand who we are and how we belong.

New forms of media have led to new forms of story-telling. For example, news reporting underwent a major transformation in the late nineteenth century when jour-nalists adopted an enduring form of news storytelling, known as the **inverted pyramid**.[7] You may be familiar with this form of reporting, even if you do not recognize the name journalists use to describe it.

In the structure of the inverted pyramid, journalists report the most important, essential facts about the story first, including who did what, and when, where, and why they did it. Often all these facts are reported in the very first sentence, in what is known as a "summary lede." As the story con-tinues, later sentences and paragraphs introduce additional details and background information in descending order of importance.

Notice how the inverted pyramid distinguishes journalism from other forms of storytelling. Most often when we share

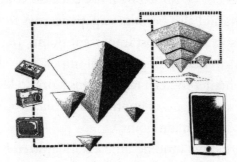

stories, we tell them in *chronological* order, building to a dramatic finale. Just as fairy tales and other fictional stories often start with standardized beginnings ("Once upon a time . . ." or "It was a dark and stormy night . . .") so, too, do many news stories. The inverted pyramid and summary lede are **conventions** in the sense that reporters, editors, and readers have a shared familiarity with them. Conventions such as the inverted pyramid make writing stories predictable for journalists and reading stories routine for readers.

Because the inverted pyramid provides a standardized format that can be used for almost any news story, regardless of its topic, reporters can quickly write a story's introduction. That is helpful because reporters often work under the pressure of tight deadlines. Because the inverted pyramid puts the most important information first and the least important information last, newspaper editors who need to shorten a story so that it fits in the space available can simply begin by cutting from the bottom of the story, confident that its most important points and overall organization will not be ruined by those cuts. Of course, the inverted pyramid also permits impatient news readers to quickly grasp a story's most important point. The organization of news in descending order of importance allows you to decide whether to keep reading this story to learn more about it or to move on to another story once you've grasped the current story's main point.

The inverted pyramid became a standardized form of

news reporting in the United States in the late nineteenth century, at the same time as the development of the telegraph and changes in how journalists understood their work.[8] The telegraph allowed news outlets to communicate information quickly along wires across long distances. But transmission time was valuable and sometimes telegraph connections failed. So telegraph messages aimed for brevity. For example, a telegraph announced the death of President Lincoln: *Abraham Lincoln died this morning at 22 minutes after seven.*[9] The inverted pyramid structure ensured that the most important facts of a story were transmitted first. In case of a lost connection, newspapers that depended on the telegraph for the latest news could still print the most important facts of the story.

But technology alone did not establish the inverted pyramid as a new form of journalism. Michael Schudson, a sociologist who studies the history of journalism in the United States, makes the case that, in addition to the telegraph, journalists' developing sense of reporting as a profession helped establish the inverted pyramid as a conventional form of news storytelling. According to Schudson, increasingly independent journalists began to assert their own authority to judge what aspect of a news story was most important.[10] They began to claim authority as experts, something previous generations of journalists had not been able to do. The inverted pyramid permitted journalists to suggest that *journalists'* judgment could be trusted as *expert* judgment.

Write a Summary Lede for a News Story of Your Own Choosing

Pick an event from your day and write a summary lede paragraph that describes it. To do so, you'll need to decide not only what to describe but also what you consider the most important element of the story. Check out the Purdue Online Writing Lab (or OWL) for tips on writing a summary lede.[128] As the Purdue OWL website states, a good lede "gives readers the most important information in a clear, concise and interesting manner."

With the development of *online* journalism, some critics say the inverted pyramid is less useful or relevant now than it was in the past. Think about Twitter as a new medium, and perhaps take three minutes to view the video interview "Twitter and the Telegraph," with the science author Ainissa Ramirez, posted online as part of season 5 of PBS's SciTechNow series.[129] Do you think the short, compressed format of communication via tweets makes Twitter the new, digital equivalent of the old telegraph?

Conventions, such as the inverted pyramid and summary lede, also make it easy to write parodies of real news stories. A parody is a literary or musical work in which the style of an author or work is closely imitated for comic effect. The people at *The Onion* are masters when it comes to writing parody news stories. Check out some made-up news stories at *The Onion* (https://www.theonion.com/) and focus on how these imitations use real news conventions (such as the summary lede and inverted pyramid) to make us laugh.

Moving beyond news and journalism, think about other forms of media and the conventions that these forms regularly use. For example, how do "mockumentaries," such as the classic *This Is Spinal Tap* (1984) or *Best in Show* (2000), construct parodies of both the documentary format as well as the topics they cover? Or how does the music of "Weird Al" Yankovic play with the conventions of songwriting to turn one song's message into something entirely different? How have these examples been used to create parodies of the original form?

If media are about storytelling, then it makes sense to ask, "*Who* are the storytellers?" A critical-media-literacy perspective suggests that we cannot fully understand media messages—the stories we tell ourselves via different media—without also examining media ownership and economic interests, including the motivation to make money.

Media Ownership

While it seems as if there are *endless* media choices, when we look more closely, we see that we have really limited options from which to choose. Yes, it seems as if TikTok videos will go on forever, and most of us have not actually watched all the options available on Netflix. But when we look closely at the business of media, we see that the choices are few. There are just a few companies that own, operate, produce, and distribute almost

all our media. As of this writing, only six companies produce more than 90 percent of the media we watch, read, and listen to.[11] When we look at digital media, including social media and online platforms, only about five companies control most of what we do online.[12]

These corporations provide us with endless entertainment, no doubt! However, they are most interested in their own bottom line—that is, their own profit. Media corporations in the United States are, for the most part, private companies, which means their primary goal is profit. They aim to make as much money as possible, and they do so by entertaining us (if we are not entertained, they will not make money)—but we are not truly their first priority. We'll discuss this more in chapter 6, where we focus on advertising.

Part of how these corporations make so much money is through our work. When you post a video to TikTok, or create a SnapStory, or post to Instagram or Facebook, you are giving your content to those corporations. If you, alone, stop doing that work, not much will change. However, if *all of us* stop posting, those sites would be empty.

These companies cannot make money without content. We provide the content, but for the most part, we do not make any money for our work. By contrast, these companies and their top executives make a *lot* of money from our work! As of 2021, Apple was a $2 trillion company; Amazon, Alphabet (the parent company of Google, which owns YouTube), and Microsoft were each worth over $1.5 trillion; and Meta (the parent company of Facebook, Instagram, and WhatsApp) was worth over $870 billion.[13]

Beyond the massive profits made by this handful of media giants, another basic concern about media ownership involves diversity. A critical-media-literacy perspective on media ownership leads us to ask, "Does a lack of diversity in media *ownership* lead to an equivalent lack of diversity in media *content?*" When a small group of corporations controls most media, how does that affect what stories get told, how those stories get told, and how widely they're shared? Maybe you've had the experience where you've watched, read, or listened to something and felt that some part of the story—maybe the part that would reflect your interests, your identity, or your experiences—had been left out. This may lead you to think more closely about diversity, especially in terms of representation.

Encoding and Decoding Media Messages

The media of entertainment come to us as carefully crafted, complete productions. They were written, produced, and distributed by teams of people. This means that they carry with them messages constructed either intentionally or unintentionally by the creators. However, we do not have to accept the intended meaning of the message. Examining how media messages are not only encoded but also decoded reminds us that audience members are active participants in the process.

The **encoding-decoding model** was first proposed by the British media scholar Stuart Hall in the early 1970s.[14] Although Hall was focused mainly on television, we can extend the model to other media. Basically, Hall argued that texts were embedded with particular messages as part of their production. As audiences, we decode those messages; that's how we make sense of the story being told. But Hall did not think that the process was one-way; that is, he did not think that we, as audiences, would limit our interpretations to *only* the encoded message.

Hall thought that audiences were active and that individual audience members would bring their own meaning to the texts. You bring your life's learning and experiences to all the media with which you engage. This is one way that you and your friends can watch the same movie or TV show, listen to the same song, or follow the same social media influencer, and still feel as if you are learning totally different things.

While media producers encode their texts with an intended meaning, you bring your own knowledge to those texts and you may accept, reject, or negotiate their intended meaning. That is, you can believe it to be true and accept

the message as is, or you can reject it and even stop engaging with it (as might be the case when you decide to turn off a specific movie or song because it does not resonate with you). But most commonly, you *negotiate* the meaning: you take elements of the encoded message and interpret them in terms of your life experience and values to construct a narrative and a response that reflects your own worldview.

Hall's encoding-decoding model challenged what had been one previously dominant understanding of media effects. The **hypodermic needle theory** explained the effects of media as if the message encoded in the content entered directly into the audience, without any chance for members of the audience to resist its influence. Hall believed that audience members could be more active participants in constructing a media message's meaning than predicted by the hypodermic needle model.

Powerful Solidarities and Fateful Divisions: Making Sense of Interpretive Communities

Hall's encoding-decoding model is especially interesting because it opens up the idea of different **interpretive communities**, a term scholars use to describe groups of people whose shared values, beliefs, experiences, and assumptions lead them to interpret the world in similar ways. Originally, the idea was developed to explain how writers and readers developed understandings of the characters in novels and how those characters should be interpreted.

When you recall that all media involve storytelling, then you can see how membership in an interpretive community could shape not only how we read stories in books but also more broadly how we "read" or decode meanings across a wide variety of media "texts." Two relevant modern examples of interpretive communities could be the fandoms or fan theories that are becoming increasingly common, such as the BTS ARMY, movie fandoms, or FaZe Clan-like gamer communities within Twitch streams, Esports, or Discord.

One benefit of thinking about media in terms of interpretive communities is that this concept reminds us that the interpretive process is simultaneously personal and social. How you interpret some specific media message is, of course, personal and potentially unique to you. However, your tastes, judgments, and values, even your perceptions and most basic assumptions, are continually being shaped by the relationships and the communities that make you who you are.

Interpretive Communities

An interpretive community is a group of people whose shared values, beliefs, and assumptions lead them to make sense of the world in similar ways.

- What interpretive communities do you belong to?
- What shared understandings help define that community?
- How do those understandings shape the way that you make sense of media?

It may be difficult to answer these questions in the abstract. Instead, select some specific media content—a particular book, movie, podcast, or social media post—and think about how one or more interpretive communities that you belong to shape your understanding of that media content.

This helps to explain how you might find yourself in agreement with your friends about the meaning of a media message, but totally at odds with your teacher or your parents about the same content. Among your peers, shared understandings based on being at a similar stage in life might unify you as an interpretive community, while also defining differences between you and your teachers or parents. Of course, interpretive communities are not necessarily based on age. They could also be based on shared gender identity and sexuality, geography, political beliefs, or socioeconomic status, to name just a few factors.

Interpretive communities are powerful forces in shaping—and potentially reshaping—our understandings of the world. A sense of shared values and interpretive frameworks can serve as bonds among a group of people, creating strong feelings of identity and solidarity within the group—just as differences (real or imagined) in values and ways of understanding can lead to disputes, and even deadly conflict, between groups.

Social scientists use the terms "in-group" and "out-group" to describe these dynamics. An **in-group** is one that a person identifies with and feels loyalty toward; by contrast, an **out-group** is one toward which a person feels opposition, rivalry, or hostility. As the sociologist Robert Merton observed, we tend to think of the groups we identify with in virtuous terms, while depicting members of out-groups as blameworthy or villainous.[15] So we might perceive members of an out-group as "lazy" (but we're "laid-back"), as "snobs" (when we're "classy"), or as "zealots" (while we're "devout").

The dynamics of in-groups and out-groups can be as obvious and commonplace as sports rivalries that organize (mostly healthy) competition between teams of opposing players and their fans, who identify on the basis of their attachment and loyalty to rival schools or cities. But in more extreme cases, in-group–out-group dynamics can align with deeply rooted prejudices and systemic discrimination to support catastrophes such as slavery and genocide.

Examining interpretive communities helps clarify how the media we use can harness and steer these group dynamics—including both the potential for powerful solidarities and the threat of fateful divisions. For example, radio broadcasts played a deadly role in the genocide in Rwanda, which took place between April and June of 1994 and resulted in an estimated 800,000 deaths. One radio station in particular, Radio Télévision Libre des Mille Collines (RTLM), played a significant role in inciting the genocide. The popular radio station broadcast hate propaganda that dehumanized members of Rwanda's Tutsi ethnic group, as well as politically moderate members of the rival Hutu ethnic group. In an extreme example of out-group vilification, RTLM consistently referred to Tutsis as "cockroaches." The hateful broadcasts urged Hutus to identify in ethnic terms, as Hutus, to join together in a "final war" to "exterminate the cockroaches."[16] The radio station went so far as to give real-time directions to where Tutsis were hiding.[17]

Recognizing the powerful role of RTLM in spurring on the killing, the US government considered jamming its radio broadcasts. After deliberation within the US Department of Defense, President Bill Clinton's deputy assistant for national security, Frank G. Wisner, wrote a memo reporting that jamming the station's broadcasts would be "an ineffective and expensive mechanism" to help stop the genocide in Rwanda.[18] By contrast, General Roméo Dallaire, commander of UN peacekeeping operations in Rwanda at the time of the genocide, subsequently stated, "Simply jamming [the] broadcasts and replacing them with messages of peace and reconciliation would have had a significant impact on the course of events."[19] In 2003, an international court convicted two of RTLM's directors for their roles in inciting the 1994 genocide.[20]

Consider a second, more recent example of interpretive communities at work in cases of violent conflict. In February 2022, Russia invaded Ukraine. Many US politicians and news outlets described Russia's military assault on Ukraine as "unprovoked." For example, in his first statement after the start of the invasion, US president Joseph Biden called the Russian attack "unprovoked and unjustified."[21] Democrats in Congress, including Senator

Elizabeth Warren, of Massachusetts, and Representative Adam Schiff, of California, also described Russia's aggression as "unprovoked."[22] Republican members of Congress did not necessarily use President Biden's language, but they joined the White House in condemning Russian president Vladimir Putin's military invasion: Representative Mike Gallagher, of Wisconsin, described Putin as "a KGB thug who understands no language except force," while the House minority leader, Kevin McCarthy, of California, characterized Putin's attack on Ukraine as "reckless and evil."[23] A number of US news outlets—including Axios, CNBC, and Vox—echoed these political leaders' descriptions of the Russian assault on Ukraine as "unprovoked."[24] These politicians and news outlets framed Russia and especially Putin as dangerous villains and Ukraine and its people as innocent victims.

Fairness & Accuracy in Reporting, a well-respected progressive media watchdog, articulated a somewhat different perspective. FAIR's Bryce Greene noted that FAIR "resolutely condemns the invasion as illegal and ruinous." However, Greene continued, "calling [the invasion] 'unprovoked' distracts attention from the US's own contribution to this disastrous outcome."[25] As Greene's article analyzed in detail, the United States "ignored warnings from both Russian and US officials that a major conflagration could erupt if the US continued its path." That path included the United States' refusals to de-escalate tensions in the region by halting expansion of NATO, to negotiate for Ukrainian neutrality in the East-West rivalry between Russia and the United States, and to remove missiles, troops, and bases near Russia. From this standpoint, although Russia's invasion still deserved condemnation, the United States also ought to be held accountable for how its own military and foreign policy positions may have provoked Putin's aggression. Taking into account US provocations, Putin's response may not seem so unpredictable or irrational.

Both these examples of media in the context of violent conflict are complex and each case merits further investigation. Here our emphasis has been on how media messages can mobilize our identities to form communities that will act in common. Usually we think of "community" and "acting in common" as wholly good things, as signals of positive connections between groups of people. But, as these examples show, the role of media in promoting—and potentially exploiting—in-group–out-group dynamics is one stark example of why critical media literacy matters. (For more on in-groups and out-groups, see the examination of "filter bubbles" in chapter 5.)

CHAPTER 2

Critical Thinking

What Is Critical Thinking?

How do we know what is true about the world? As we spend more and more time on our screens, we are inundated with more and more media messages. What does all this information mean? Where does it come from? How do we know whether the things we see, hear, or read are real? What questions do we ask to verify information? Media citizens are able to answer these questions by thinking critically. In this chapter, we introduce key concepts for understanding what it means to think critically. Being critical means you ask basic questions, much as a detective would when trying to solve a crime.

By the way, being a critical thinker does not mean you have some magic potion for truth-seeking. Critical thinkers still struggle with evaluating information and even the best critical thinkers are sometimes fooled by the media's messages. Critical thinkers do at least one distinct thing that sets them apart: they keep asking questions, even if (especially when!) they may stumble over the answers.

This chapter introduces some of the terms and definitions that will be used later in this book and that you may encounter in your daily lives. They'll help you build a solid foundation for better understanding of both your media use and your interpersonal interactions. Think of this chapter as a reference for when you are looking to better understand what can happen when a media text, a friend, or a family member introduces a new, potentially controversial, topic. The material in this chapter will help you become a more informed critical thinker.

Critical thinking is a process that leads us to rational, evidence-based understanding of what is happening in the world. Critical thinking refers to "general strategies" people use "to gather and evaluate data, generate hypotheses, assess evidence and arrive at conclusions."[26] Asking questions is fundamental to critical thinking. As a critical thinker, you seek knowledge, make and analyze arguments, evaluate evidence, recognize bias, and strive for objectivity. Critical thinkers assert four primary values: autonomy, curiosity, humility, and respect.[27] By engaging with these primary values you can make more persuasive arguments.

An **argument** refers to a claim that leads to a conclusion. These claims are based on a series of inferences and supported by evidence. It is important to note that an argument is not the same as a fight. An argument establishes a position on a given topic, supported by evidence that we articulate through dialogue. The process of building an argument is a construction zone, not a combat zone. The purpose is to increase understanding, not hostility. A sound, logical argument is like a well-constructed building. None of the components are independent; they all support and are supported by other components of the argument. If they are deemed to be well supported, then the argument is logical. **Logic** refers to the process and assessment of reasoning in accordance with strict principles of **validity**.[28] A weak foundation or unstable footing results in a shaky building, which might be condemned as unsafe. Similarly, baseless claims and weak evidence result in a feeble argument, which might be dismissed as illogical. Think about a time when you asked your parent or guardian for something, such as more screen time, a later curfew, or perhaps to get your nose pierced. Chances are, if you yelled and screamed, they were less inclined to listen. But if you presented your ideas with a well-thought-out plan (more screen time as a well-deserved reward for good grades; a later curfew in exchange for an additional chore to illustrate how responsible you are; a nose piercing from a safe place, with a clear health record), they may have been more inclined to listen and to engage in a conversation.

The foundation of critical thinking involves acquiring knowledge. **Knowledge** refers to the facts, information, and skills obtained through experience or education that provide us with understanding of a subject. A **fact** is veri-

fiable. A fact is beyond argument. A fact is different from an **opinion**, which is an attempt to draw an honest judgment based upon the facts. Facts and opinions both differ from a **belief**, which is a conviction based on something other than evidence, such as faith, morals, or values. Beliefs cannot be disproven, because they do not rest on evidence.

For example, your opinion may be that TikTok is a better platform than Facebook or you may believe that your day is better when you watch television in the morning. These are not based on objective evidence, but preferences, feelings, and other tastes that cannot be confirmed. Similarly, your cell phone can report how long you spend on an app such as Snapchat (a matter of fact). But you may have different views than your parents or guardians about how much time you *should* spend on the app (a matter of opinion).

Making a Good Argument

Critical thinkers construct arguments to persuade others, to help them to see what we see in the world around us. Given what we just stated about knowledge, facts, opinions, and beliefs, it is important that you understand how these concepts work together. A critical thinker accumulates knowledge through facts, and then forms an opinion based on those facts. This process may even lead us to challenge and change our own belief system! Therefore, part of critical thinking is self-reflection: What do I know and how do I know it? What do I believe and why do I believe it? The more familiar we are with our own beliefs, the more we may be able to articulate them clearly.

The first major part of any argument is the claim. A **claim** asserts the truth of something, but is typically disputed or in doubt. For example, say you make the claim that *every time* you are on YouTube, you see unboxing videos, which feature people opening packages of items they just purchased and showing off the products. But, if you go on YouTube one time and don't see an unboxing video, the claim is untrue. To avoid false claims such as these, critical thinkers use qualifiers. A **qualifier** is a word or phrase that modifies how certain, absolute, or generalizable a statement is. Rather than saying "YouTube *always* recommends unboxing videos to me," you would replace *always* with the qualifier *often*: "YouTube *often* suggests unboxing videos." Being careful with our own language and word choices can help us evaluate others' language and word choices, which, in turn, may help us to be more informed media citizens.

In order to determine the veracity of the claim and its qualifiers, critical thinkers evaluate the available evidence.

Evidence refers to the known facts and information available to test a claim. Without evidence the claim cannot be evaluated, which means there is no argument to be made. For example, people may recommend or discourage a product without reason. However, this does not supply you with evidence for why a product works or how. Did the person giving the review get a bad batch? Or are they being paid to promote it? Without evidence, you do not know. There are generally three types of evidence: primary, secondary, and tertiary sources. A **primary source** is evidence from an original source, such as an eyewitness account or historic document. A **secondary source** is evidence that derives from somewhere other than the original, such as someone repeating what they heard from an eyewitness or commenting on a primary source. A **tertiary source** is a thirdhand source of evidence, one that collates and summarizes primary and secondary sources, often for instructional purposes. For example, the book you are reading right now is a tertiary source.[29] It contains examples from secondary and primary sources, but does not offer direct access to those sources.

Avoiding Common Fallacies

A lack of agreement between the evidence and the claim is known as a fallacy. A **fallacy** is a faulty or inaccurate claim made based on the evidence or lack thereof. For example, if a classmate tells you that you need to get the new smartphone because everyone is getting it right now, this is a bandwagon fallacy. Or if a commercial tells you that Brand X is the best clothing because the pop star Dua Lipa says so, that is an appeal-to-authority fallacy. Fallacies can be mistakes in reasoning, or they can be used deliberately as a form of **propaganda** to cajole or trick an audience. Common informal logical fallacies include the following:[30]

Ad Hominem: Attacking a person or source rather than addressing the argument being made (*ad hominem* means "to the person" in Latin)

Appeal to Authority: Believing claims because an alleged expert is cited in argument

Appeal to Emotion: Exploiting emotional entanglements to build support for an argument

Appeal to Ignorance: Preying on one's lack of knowledge regarding a particular topic

Bandwagon / Ad Populum: Believing something is true because a majority of people agree

Begging the Question / Circular Reasoning: Restating a premise as a conclusion without evidence

Correlation Fallacy: Asserting that correlation implies causation. This is sometimes referred to as a "post hoc fallacy": because Event Y followed Event X, X must have caused Y

False Analogy: Comparing unlike things as though they were more related than they are

False Dilemma: Forcing an option between two choices when there are multiple alternatives (also referred to as the either-or fallacy)

Halo Effect: Assigning positive attributes to a source based on one issue or situation

Hasty Generalization: Jumping to a conclusion based on a limited or weak observation

Red Herring: Changing the topic of an argument for strategic purposes

Slippery Slope: Claiming that because one negative thing may occur, others will automatically follow

Straw Person: Distorting someone's argument or viewpoint so it is easier to tear apart or refute

Sweeping Generalization: Casting inclusive categorization for complicated or diverse things

Wishful Thinking: Convincing oneself that something is true, regardless of what the evidence suggests, simply because one wants it to be true

We know that's a long list—and you may not encounter many of those terms on a regular basis. However, having this information available may help inform some of the choices you make. To apply your knowledge, and determine the veracity of a claim, critical thinkers first examine the evidence behind the claim, ask relevant questions, and then move toward a conclusion. To refer back to the first example in this chapter, maybe now that you have seen this list of fallacies, you have a better understanding of why your initial ask for more screen time, a later curfew, or a pierced nose was met with a hard "no" from your parents or guardians. Were you engaging in wishful thinking or sweeping generalizations? We have definitely all been there!

What Are Inferences?

An inference is a conclusion based on evidence and reasoning. **Reasoning** refers to a set of processes that serve as problem-solving tools; reasoning helps us "go beyond the information given."[31] In our everyday lives, we use informal reasoning to make practical decisions, such as "We should leave early because the restaurant gets crowded at noon." Critical thinkers apply reasoning to evidence and draw inferences. An **inference** produces a conclusion based on available information. There are three main types of inferences: deductive, inductive, and abductive.

A **deductive inference** involves reaching a logical conclusion based on the relationship between the premise and the conclusion: if we determine that the premise is true, then we accept that the conclusion must also be true. For example, humans are mortal and you are a human, so you must be mortal. An **inductive inference** is based on a sample where broad generalizations are drawn from observable information. Inductive reasoning relies on probability to draw an inference based on observed patterns. So if you selected one of your followers on Instagram and they are the same age as you, through inductive inference you might conclude, "Since the follower I selected is the same age as I am, most likely I have other followers the same age as well." An **abductive inference** relies on an incomplete set of observations and chooses the likeliest one to draw a conclusion. Say you wake up for school one morning and your phone's weather app says it will rain today. You grab your jacket, and then, browsing your social media feed, you see a picture of a friend wearing a tank top to school with a caption indicating that they are expecting sunshine and high temperatures. You would need to use abductive inference—deciding which claim is more likely to be true—to determine whether or not you should bring a jacket

Inferences must also be valid. The **validity** of an inference refers to the certainty about the truth of the inference based on empirical evidence. This is to say that in addition to confidence, the question of knowledge depends upon factual truth. Chances are good that you do a lot of the types of reasoning just described without even consciously thinking about it. (Can you imagine if we had to pause and detail every thought process we have throughout the day? We would never get anything done!) We share these definitions and examples as a way to name what you are probably already doing.

Objectivity and Recognizing Cognitive Biases and Their Effects

In order to ensure that we are not swayed by self-serving explanations and interests, critical thinkers strive for objectivity. **Objectivity** denotes impartial and balanced thinking about the evidence. This means you decide what is true based on evidence, rather than what you want to be true. For example, you may want school to be canceled tomorrow, and your friend may tell you that it is, but you cannot ignore that your teacher told you school is not canceled. Objectivity differs from **subjective thinking**, which is based on one's feelings and preferences. Objective thinkers try to reduce the influence of their biases on their conclusions. A **cognitive bias** refers to someone's prejudice or inclination. It is often difficult for us to see our own biases, which makes them more challenging to address. Biases become problematic when they lead us to deviate from a rational thought process or the truth.

Biases can work to undermine critical thinking, especially when you run into information or an argument with which you are unfamiliar. Bias may lead you to automatically dismiss an idea rather than engage it or explore new, different perspectives. **Cognitive dissonance** is the state of psychic discomfort that occurs when you encounter information that contradicts your preexisting beliefs or ideas. Running into cognitive dissonance is like arriving at a crossroads.

On one path, you have an opportunity to engage a topic or argument using your critical thinking skills; alternatively, down a different path, you could ignore the challenging idea or information and simply double down on your pre-conceived notions.

For example, many of us care about the environment and human rights, but our smartphones depend on rare minerals, including coltan, that can only be obtained by mining opera-tions that harm the environment and result in human rights abuses. Learning about how our smartphones connect us to human exploitation or environmental degradation can create the unpleasant stress or confusion of cognitive dissonance.

Other biases—such as **dissonance reduction**—work to alleviate such mental discomfort, but dissonance reduction is unlikely to lead to the best possible or most reasoned conclusions. In fact, it often motivates people to do the opposite.[32] For example, to reduce the dissonance that results from learning about the harmful effects of buying a smartphone, you may reason with yourself by rationalizing that you simply *had* to make the purchase, because your other phone had broken and it is impractical to go without a mobile phone these days. This may help to lessen the uncomfortable feelings that come with new knowledge, but it does not offer a conclusion that prevents environmental damage or human rights violations. Rather, it helps justify our choice in the moment (and may serve to excuse future smartphone purchases). Some argue that it is impossible to completely remove bias, so we should at least be familiar with some common types of cognitive bias and how they impact our thinking.

Unconscious or Implicit Bias refers to how we "unknowingly draw upon assumptions about individuals and groups to make decisions about them."[33] Essentially, it refers to biases about which we are not aware. The psychologist Jennifer L. Eberhardt, author of *Biased: Uncovering the Hidden Prejudice That Shapes What We See, Think, and Do*, focuses on the role implicit bias plays in racism. She says, "We all have ideas about race, even the most open-minded among us. Those ideas have the power to bias our perception, our attention, our memory and our actions—all despite our conscious or deliberate intentions. Our ideas about race are shaped by the stereotypes to which we are exposed on a daily basis. . . . Confronting implicit bias requires we look in the mirror."[34] For example, research has shown that African Americans and Latinos are more likely to be shown as "lawbreakers" in news media. How does this reinforce a harmful stereotype of people of color as criminals? How might this create or fortify implicit bias?

Confirmation Bias refers to a preference for information that agrees with our preexisting beliefs while ignoring contrary evidence. This is one of the most common forms of bias, closely linked to other specific effects of biases including motivated reasoning, inferred justification, and succumbing to pseudoscience.

Self-Serving Bias is a practice in which individuals attribute positive outcomes to their own behavior and negative outcomes to others. For example, when a student fails a test they may blame the teacher, but if they pass it they credit themselves. Or if a political candidate wins an election, the candidate claims the victory was due to their superior policy positions and popularity, but if they lose, they say the process was unfair or rigged.

Curse-of-Knowledge Bias is displayed when an individual assumes that everyone should know what *they* know. This is flawed logic because it ignores the learning process. The curse-of-knowledge bias is clearly on display when, for example, people claim how obvious a conclusion is now, even though they just learned to see it that way recently.

Hindsight Bias occurs when individuals claim that an outcome was obvious because they know what happened. The phrase "hindsight is 20/20" refers to the fact that outcomes can seem obvious once they have occurred, even though the outcome may not have been previously obvious or predictable. This bias is sometimes referred to as "armchair quarterbacking."

Optimism-Pessimism Bias occurs when individuals' predictions about a negative or positive outcome reflect the positive or negative feelings they have at that particular moment. It is a form of emotional bias that can be very influential in how someone arrives at a particular position. Political campaigns often exploit this type of bias. For example, campaign slogans such "hope and change" or "build back better" promise better times ahead but also insert an emotional bias into the present moment.

Declinism Bias refers to the contention that the past was better than the present. For example, many people claim that social media are dividing the United States. However, over two thousand years ago, the Greek philosopher Socrates said the same thing about the written word. People are prone to recall the past with "rose-colored glasses" (as if it was better than it actually was) and to wish for a return to a prior "golden age," without taking into account past problems. This bias can manifest in interesting ways. For example, Donald Trump's campaign slogan MAGA, "Make America Great Again," appealed to a mythic version of a better period in the history of the United States, as did speeches by previous presidents (whether Democrats or Republicans), including John F. Kennedy, Ronald Reagan, and Barack Obama.

In-Group Bias occurs when an individual displays a tendency to say favorable things about a person based solely on the fact that they are members of the same group. Political partisans do this routinely, which can lead to double standards, one for those in the group, another for those outside the group. Understanding how this bias works is an important component of achieving fairness in judgment. For example, many national governments accuse other nations of conducting torture or engaging in other human rights violations, while insisting that their own conduct is law-abiding and ethical. As the late comedian and social critic George Carlin once reminded us, "Let's not have a double standard here, one standard will do just fine."

Social scientists and psychologists have noted specific, measured effects that result from the cognitive biases just introduced. One such effect is the **Forer effect** (also known as the Barnum effect), which refers to the practice of personalizing vague information to oneself without considering how it might be applied to anyone. For example, some people believe horoscopes offer unique guidance for their individual lives. Similarly, many popular personality tests produce generalized results, which people take as providing individualized insights. And yet, in both cases, the findings might apply to most people. These studies were done by the psychologist Bertram Forer in the mid-twentieth century and referred to intellectual gimmicks used by the showman P. T. Barnum for entertaining audiences in the late nineteenth century.

Another consequence of cognitive bias is referred to as the **Dunning-Kruger effect**. In this case, people with more knowledge about a topic act with caution when discussing the topic, noting its complexity, while those with less knowledge treat the topic simplistically, acting as if they have more knowledge than they do. More specifically, studies done by David Dunning and Justin Kruger in 1999 found that people with low levels of knowledge overestimate their competency in those given areas. In other words, they do not see their own limitations, leading not only to mistakes but also to failures to correct those mistakes, or even to recognize them in the first place. Politicians frequently exhibit this effect in campaign speeches or policy debates, which can lead to negative societal impacts.

We noted earlier that confirmation bias was one of the most pervasive forms of cognitive bias. Confirmation biases often manifest in what are referred to as motivated reasoning or inferred justification. **Motivated reasoning** is defined as an individuals' tendency to consider and evaluate evidence in a way that allows only for their preferred conclusion.[35] Similarly, **inferred justification** implies that we assume there must be a reason or several reasons why a particular event has taken place. This often takes the form of explaining an event based on value assumptions and confirmation bias rather than factual information. For example, the sociologist Steven Hoffman and a team of researchers highlighted this behavior in a major study looking at post-9/11 America, the war in Iraq, and claims that Iraq possessed weapons of mass destruction (WMDs). The study, titled "There Must Be a Reason: Osama, Saddam, and Inferred Justification," looked at how Americans rationalized the 2003 invasion of Iraq, even though international investigators had found no evidence of Iraqi WMDs. The researchers concluded, "People were basically making up justifications for the fact that we were at war," and the study showed how motivated reasoning and inferred justification posed a "serious challenge to democratic theory and practice."[36]

One final concept to introduce is pseudoscience. The noted astrophysicist and author Carl Sagan warned that increased reliance on pseudoscience is one major symptom of a society in cognitive decline. **Pseudoscience** relies on results that utilize opinions, beliefs, or practices that are introduced as facts, but were not arrived at by using the scientific method. As a result, arguments based on pseudoscience are often at odds with empirical reality. For example, after cherry-picking and misinterpreting historical evidence about the Mayan

calendar, many were led to believe that the world was going to end in 2012. Well, the world did not end, but that has not put an end to popular pseudoscientific beliefs. In his 1995 book, *The Demon-Haunted World*, Sagan wrote, "I have a foreboding of an America in my children's or grandchildren's time . . . when the people have lost the ability to set their own agendas or knowledgeably question those in authority; when, clutching our crystals and nervously consulting our horoscopes, our critical faculties in decline, unable to distinguish between what feels good and what's true, we slide, almost without noticing, back into superstition and darkness."[37]

This prescient observation has manifest in the current

concept of **post-truth**, which the Oxford English Dictionary declared its 2016 Word of the Year due to the concept's cultural significance.[38] Noting that the term had become "a mainstay in political commentary," Oxford defined "post-truth" as "relating to or denoting circumstances in which objective facts are less influential in shaping public opinion than appeals to emotion and personal belief."

Biases and their effects are influential on individuals' decision-making processes. Most fundamentally, biases inform our perception of reality. Biases also influence our attitudes and behaviors, which, in turn, may shape how friendly or receptive we are to others. For example, let's say you and your family went to Paris on vacation last summer and you absolutely loved it. Today, a friend told you their family would be traveling to Paris for vacation; you might be excited for your friend's trip and your own experience may bias you toward friendly encouragement, tips on top spots to visit, and great food to eat. It is also entirely possible that you have never been to Paris and when your friend tells you they will be traveling, you may be biased to simply shrug your shoulders, because a visit to Paris does not mean much to you. Biases guide our attention. Our biases can inform and filter which aspects of a person or event we focus on or ignore. Bias acts as a hindrance to logically sound argumentation. Our ability to recognize and mitigate bias in ourselves and others is the result of critical thinking, and contributes to more informed public discourse.

Applying Critical-Thinking Skills to Media

So far, what we've discussed in this chapter has focused on your thinking processes and the ways you provide and assess evidence. There are a lot of steps to critical thinking, many of which overlap with how we make sense of the media. Now that we have outlined some basic concepts of critical thinking, the construction of arguments, and how to recognize common fallacies and biases, we want to apply these to media messages. One way to apply critical thinking is through critical media literacy, the focus of our next chapter. Because we encounter so much of the world through media, and media use takes up so much of our time, we think it is important for you to have a comprehensive, holistic understanding of the media. Using critical-thinking skills to deconstruct both our own thoughts and questions as well as the information we learn from the media may help us understand the world a bit more thoroughly.

CHAPTER 3

Critical Media Literacy

Defining Critical Media Literacy

Maybe when you hear the word "critical," you think of negative stuff: to be critical *must* mean that you dislike something, right? Not always! "Critical" can be used in a variety of ways, including thinking carefully about something (critical thinking), asking questions of something (critical inquiry), and practicing media literacy (critical media literacy).

So, what's *critical* about critical media literacy (CML)? Trust us, this is *not* an order to "eat your spinach!" or to ignore media that bring you joy and happiness. Instead, as we noted in the introduction, what's critical about CML is taking a bit of distance from our media choices to examine them more thoroughly. Instead of looking only *at* our screens, we want to look *behind* the screens (or behind the scenes) to understand how the content got to us.

There are a few different ways to understand how media literacy is taught in schools in the United States. Many US schools teach media through a **protectionist** position—that is, teaching us that the media are bad for us. Protectionists are often concerned with media content they find dangerous, such as representations that glamorize violence, sex, or drug and alcohol use. They assume that once you learn that the media are bad, you will choose to turn them off. However, you know that an easy way around this is to talk upfront about how you agree these media are bad—and then use them anyway. That's one reason why we do not believe in the protectionist position: sure, there is plenty of "bad" media content out there—and some of us get really bothered by representations of violence, sex, and drug and alcohol use—but we do not think labeling content as "bad" will solve any problems or, quite frankly, teach us very much.

We also disagree with this position because it does not consider your own knowledge. This position tends to assume you are too young, naïve, or impressionable to know better. We disagree! We think you know enough to make informed judgments of your own.

Another way of studying the media in the United States appears at first to be the polar opposite of protectionism: a celebration of media. This position, as its name implies, *celebrates* media use. In the **celebratory** position, you are considered an active agent and your knowledge and media use are rewarded. In practice, advocates of a celebratory approach to media literacy have focused mainly on interactive media, such as computer games, or material you may create for your social media profiles.

One thing we like about this position is that it acknowledges that what you *do* with media matters. Scholars of this position see you as active, engaged participants in your media choices. By contrast, however, one problem with this position is that it does not offer you much information about your media choices—it just assumes they are all good. It also assumes that young people all have equal access to media, and we know this is not true. Some of you  may not have regular internet access or your own computers, which means you may not be deeply involved in creating media. Or perhaps you're just not interested in producing media and would rather be a receiver. Maybe you also sometimes feel frustrated by the media that is available to you. When we celebrate something, we generally do not ask too many questions, which means we ultimately know less about it.

The protectionist and celebrationist positions seem like opposites of each other, but they actually have a fair amount in common. Both expend a lot of energy on the content of the media—what's on the screen—without much attention, if any, on how that content came to be. Both believe that young people ought to make "better" media choices—but each position offers only a partial story about the media you use.

Both are missing a serious investigation into the **means of production**—that is, how that media content came to be. Neither position addresses the **political economy** of media analysis—the study of media ownership, production, and distribution.

Instead, both protectionist and celebrationist positions assume that once you learn about the media, you will change your behavior. The protectionists assume you will turn off all media; the celebrationists assume you will regularly embrace participatory, interactive media. We think this is a false dilemma. You can learn about the media and be media literate, but not change your actions or choices. A critically media-literate citizen is empowered to decide if they want to change their actions or not. In fact, we believe that the more media literate you are, the more you may see both the problems and the pleasures of the media, and you may choose to spend more time with media in order to keep up your learning. A potential key change is that you may be asking more questions of the media than you did before.

Critical Media Literacy

Despite their differences, protectionism and celebration share an important commonality: they both focus primarily on content and representation.

For both protectionism and celebration, media content is often approached as individual products, and these are often explored in isolation. For example, you might be involved in a discussion about a particular scene in a movie where you may talk about the dialogue between the characters or the lighting or sound effects. While that is important, it should not be the entire conversation. Critical media literacy will ask you to think about how that scene fits into the movie as a whole. It will also ask how you accessed that movie (did you watch it in a movie theater? on a streaming service? on a particular device?). CML will also ask you to think about when the movie was originally released, which may include a discussion of current events. CML will ask who wrote, produced, and distributed the movie—and, by extension, might ask what else those people and production companies had written, produced, and distributed. CML, therefore, fills in the gaps in representation.

As you can see from all these questions, CML is inquiry-based. What we do in CML is ask a *lot* of questions about our media use. We ask questions about many topics, including gender, race, class, and sexuality. Most importantly, we ask questions about power: Who has it and what they do with it, as well as who does not have it and why not. That is one reason why we ask questions about ownership, production, and distribution: because that's where much of the power of media originates. Sure, we like to watch celebrities and influencers, but while they are public faces, the team working behind the scenes has just as much, if not more, influence on the content. Social media influencers often have a team of people working for them who

Behind the Content

What was the last movie, TV show, or song you watched or listened to? Go back to that text and spend some time asking yourself the following questions about it:

- ◘ Who wrote this script or song?
- ◘ How was it distributed?
- ◘ What other media do these folks work with?
- ◘ How did you watch or listen to this text?
- ◘ What did you know about this text before we asked you these questions, and what have you learned since?

handle their "brand management," making sure that the products they endorse or the messages they send share a consistent message.

CML invites us all to be more informed in our attention to the media, which is why it is so focused on asking questions. In fact, in CML we are often less concerned with the answers and more concerned with continuously asking questions. We might think that "getting the right answer" is the most important part. This is not always the case. Because the media industries want our constant attention, it is often in *their* best interest for us to remain ignorant of certain information, so they work hard to make sure we cannot learn about particular topics. In CML, if we run into an insurmountable obstacle—if we get to a point where we are really stumped when trying to learn something—that might be a place where we pause and ask ourselves whether this could be on purpose. That is, could the corporation in charge of this text I am analyzing want me to *not* ask any more questions?

CML addresses questions of power, inequality, and the "politics of representation" in relation to filtering, misinformation, and disinformation in their many forms. This involves asking, "Who has the power to produce, distribute, and promote media messages?" We all have the power to create messages, but some of us—such as big-tech companies and large media organizations—have the power and influence to spread messages millions of times further and faster than the average media user.

Who Manages Whom?

Who is your favorite (or least favorite!) celebrity or influencer on social media? How often does their content include messages, advertisements, or links to other posts?

Do some research on their management team and the brands they work for or endorse:

◘ What can you learn about the team that works on their behalf?

◘ Do they represent any other celebrities or influencers that you know?

◘ What type of message or "brand" do you think they are trying to convey?

You can even take this one step further: investigate the brands that these celebrities or influencers endorse, and see whether you can find out who owns or operates these companies.

Representation

CML also asks, "How are individuals and identities represented in the media?" Chapter 4 discusses representations in depth, so for now we'll give just a brief introduction. This involves analyzing **stereotypes**, which are overgeneralizations or fixed beliefs about a certain group. These include xenophobic stereotypes, such as the "Arab terrorist"; sexist ones, such as the "dumb blonde girl"; and racist ones, such as the "Black criminal," to name a few obvious examples. The contemporary use of this term tracks back to Walter Lippmann, a giant of twentieth-century journalism and a pioneer of contemporary media studies.

In *Public Opinion* (1922), Lippmann defined stereotypes as "pictures in our head" that are generally resistant to change: "There is nothing so obdurate to education or to criticism as the stereotype. It stamps itself upon the evidence in the very act of securing the evidence."[39] While his words are a bit fancy (trust us, we, too, struggle with "obdurate," which is a

synonym for "inflexible" or "unyielding"), he is saying that stereotypes are powerful, even when we do not think they are, and once we believe a stereotype is true, it can be amazingly difficult to change our beliefs. Part of the work of CML

Stereotypes

Stereotypes involve judgments based on preconceived generalizations about a group or category of people.

◘ What types of stereotypes have you encountered, online or in real life?

◘ Are there any stereotypes that affect you as an individual?

◘ Can you think of any stereotypes that are beneficial or positive?

◘ Whom do these stereotypes benefit? Who do you think is in charge of producing these messages?

◘ How do you think the messages end up taking so much space online?

is to help us ask questions about our beliefs in order to learn where they came from.

CML also asks, "Who has the power to determine those representations and for what purpose?" There are a small group of influential media makers who choose to disseminate these stereotypes. CML asks media users to investigate who these media makers are and how the perpetuation of stereotypes serve their interests.

In addition to the politics of representation, CML investigates the power dynamics that shape the veracity of messages. CML asks, "Are the messages **misinformation** (which means they are false or misleading) or are they **disinformation** (which means they were *intended* to be false or misleading)?" CML does not stop at determining the veracity of a message; instead, it pursues deeper questions about why the message was created and whose interests it serves. Put another way, why did the media maker create this false message? False messages may be a tool of **propaganda**, which aims to persuade us to believe, or disbelieve, a particular message as a way of changing our behavior. We discuss propaganda further in chapter 7.

To Be Critical Does *Not* Mean to Be Negative

As we have previously stated, the term "critical" is often treated as the equivalent of "negative." The assumption is that people who are critical of the media dislike it. This is not always the case. CML is not about forcing us all to dislike the media. Rather, it is about all of us taking a step back and examining our chosen texts from a bit of a distance, to be able to look at something specific in its larger context. For example, think about some of your favorite media; maybe a book, a song, or a social media account that you follow. What do you like about that author or artist? What do you know about the posts on that account—and is it possible you could learn more about them? To be critical of media is, at the start, to learn as much about it as we possibly can. And sometimes, even when we really like something, we may also be able to recognize that there are some things about it that could be improved. We want to learn more about the whole text. Remember the first few paragraphs of this book? What we want to do is look closely at the inner workings of the clock and learn how its component pieces work. This is the process of critical inquiry, a part of critical thinking.

We cannot learn this information in isolation. Part of critical thinking and critical inquiry is to be in dialogue with our friends, families, classmates, and community members. We might all view the same text in slightly different ways, but the more we engage with each other and talk about the various ways that we make sense of the media, the more we will learn about it. This is a social process, and is part of the encoding-decoding process discussed in chapter 1.

CML is not hyper-focused on making sure you get the "right" answer. We have all been in those classes or taken those tests where there is one, single correct answer. This is valuable sometimes—for example, in math, it can be pretty important to know the precise solution, and in history sometimes the specific dates are undeniably significant. But in CML, we're really more focused on understanding our media texts in context and how our own positions intersect with each other (or not!). For example, we live in a technological world where we can watch a show on a television, on a tablet or computer, on a smartphone, or on any one of these devices while on an airplane. Therefore, that TV show is not *just* a TV show. It is also a way of understanding how we access our media and how our media are organized. In CML, we pay close attention to the content of media while we also work to understand where that content sits.

CML is a **liberatory** approach to making sense of the world. CML seeks to equip people with the tools to be independent media users, free from oppression or restrictions by others. We recognize that misinformation, disinformation, stereotypes, and problematic representations exist, but as media users we do *not* have to accept or internalize them. Instead, we can expose, question, and oppose them. Indeed, an important part of being critically media literate involves creating media. Rather than just noting the problems with the media we encounter, CML encourages users to liberate themselves by creating the messages and representations they wish they found in dominant media. This has the dual effect of honing your CML skills and liberating others from being controlled by the **hegemonic** messages of dominant media. In the introduction, we brought up the Universal Declaration of Human Rights and its vision of freedom of opinion and freedom of expression as inalienable rights. Developing ideas of your own and expressing them through media can be one way to transform those lofty ideals into real action. Social media, for example, have been shown to be useful platforms for calling out creators whose content is harmful or inaccurate.

Not Just One Thing

In this chapter, we've shared the definitions and some applications of critical media literacy. CML is about taking a step back from our media choices—our media of entertainment, our media of information, and the media to which we are exposed just by living in the world—in order to understand them better. But critical media literacy is not just one thing. It's multifaceted, because the world we live in and the media we use are diverse and complex. Think about the different aspects of your identity: *you* are not just one thing either. By addressing representation, CML helps expand our understanding of identity.

CHAPTER 4

Representation

What Is Representation?

Media in all its forms—visual and aural, print and digital, fiction and nonfiction—tell us some sort of story. But, instead of telling us all of a story's micro-details (which would probably bore us), media producers employ symbolism to help their audiences understand a complete, meaningful story. For the most part, once we become familiar with the basic codes and conventions of different media, we can predict some things about each story we watch: the "good" character will typically triumph in the end, while the "bad" one will be punished accordingly; two people who have somehow been separated will conventionally reunite and fall in love; adventures will be completed successfully and problems will be solved, all by the time the credits roll (or the song ends, or the book is done, . . . you get the idea).

Representations in the media teach us about ourselves and others, how we interact in the world, and how we are seen and understood (or misunderstood), based on how we are depicted. We can also look at representation through its absence: what we *see* tells one story; what we *do not* see (that is, what is ignored or downplayed by the media) tells a different, equally important story. The media tell stories that give us, and others, a sense of who we are as people and how the multiple components of our identities matter.

Why We Are Influenced by Media Representations

This chapter investigates the cyclical nature of representation in the media. This cycle starts when media messages reflect socially constructed elements of society. This can then lead to the creation of narrow or stereotypical content. As consumers, we come next in the cycle, unconsciously (or consciously, after reading this book!) interpreting what we see in the media in terms of our everyday experience. Then society at large reflects the culmination of attitudes and actions of individuals like yourself.

And so the cycle starts all over again, as media content continues to rely on generalized interpretations of the world around us. Now, this is not necessarily a rigid cycle; quite the opposite! CML provides us with the tools to see these patterns and act as conscious users to call out inadequate representations or to form our own understandings of society, independent of media influence.

How do we make sense of the world around us? Our identities are shaped by ourselves and from outside influences, such as what we learn from our parents, in the classroom, from friends, from our community, and maybe from our faith. All sorts of systems in our lives work together to form our understanding of who we are, and to develop the ways we make meaning of people, places, and concepts. The media also play a big role in shaping our identities. The media have the power to inform us about all sorts of things we may not be able to directly experience in real life.

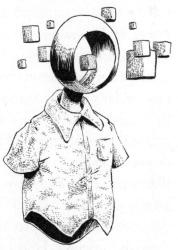

Critical thinking encourages us to see that media representations are *not* reality; rather they are reflections or replications of social constructs that exist in real life. **Social constructs** tell us how society (the "social") has assigned meaning (the "construct") to objective reality. These constructs can shape our understanding of matters such as race, gender and sexuality, ability, and many other facets of individual or group identities.

Since the media cannot possibly capture *every* intricate aspect of our society, media draw on these established social constructs to shape what they represent (and *do not* represent) and how they represent it. When our lens on the world is influenced too much by what we see, hear, or read in the media, we risk missing the full picture.

You may already understand that media representations do not always coincide with reality. Recalling our discussion of Stuart Hall's encoding-decoding model in chapter 1, we can now appreciate more about why "decoding" media representations is so important. Media consumers have a dual ability to know something is not real and yet still have a very authentic, visceral reaction to the content. For example, you may jump out of your seat when a ghost appears in a scary movie or cry when your favorite character dies in a television show. Nonfiction and news media can similarly shape our attitudes, even with the knowledge that their "reality" is one constructed for us, not uniquely representative of the world at large. For example, you may be conscious of the fact that millions of successful airplane flights take place every day, yet still feel anxious when flying after hearing about a plane crash on the news. Media have the power to create representations that *feel* real to users through conscious choices of visuals, sounds, phrases, and other elements. In other words, the media are a powerful tool for crafting how we feel, act, and interact with the world.

The media scholar Stuart Hall offers a framework for understanding just how powerful the media are in constructing ideologies, or the various systems through which we characterize, and comprehend, elements of society. The media act as "part of the dominant means of ideological production" because of their unique ability to create and shape how we view aspects of the world around us.[40] Throughout history, media have often failed to be entirely equal, fair, or inclusive in their representations of identities such as race, sexuality, gender, class, ability, family structure, and language usage. Looking through a critical lens helps us to question *whom* or *what* the media choose to represent (or not represent). *How* are these represented? And *why*?

How Media Construct Representations: Visibility, Framing, and Stereotypes

As previously noted, representation is important to analyze both in terms of what the media show and what the media *do not* show. One way that we can do this is by assessing visibility. In 1934, Hollywood cinema began enforcing the Motion Picture Production Code, a set of guidelines to censor visual media. These rules prohibited showing any relationships or content that strayed from "traditional" values of that era. The code banned depictions of homosexuality, interracial romance, violence, and more. Hollywood did away with this ancient set of rules more than fifty years ago, but contemporary media content still struggles to provide adequate visibility to contemporary representations of gender, sexuality, race, class, ability, and family structure. We may have more diverse representations in media today than we did fifty years ago, but visibility is not just about quantity. Yes, we may see a more complex set of characters in our media, but what is the quality of their representation? Both the quantity and the quality of representation deserve to be analyzed.

Investigating visibility as a media citizen also means looking closer at *how* media fail, or succeed, in representing the complexities of our identities and individual experiences. Imagine yourself standing in the middle of an intersection. There are roads in front of you, behind you, to the left and to the right of you. Now picture each of these intersecting roads as individual representations of your identity. One road may represent your race, the other your gender, and so on. Scholars in Black feminism, such as Patricia Hill Collins and Kimberlé Crenshaw, have investigated this crossroad of identity components through **intersectionality**, where multiple types of disadvantage or discrimination can occur.[41] Addressing, or giving visibility to, different identity categories in isolation fails to consider their overlap in real life, and, therefore, the overlap of oppressions faced by many. When you watch a movie, see an advertisement, or interact with any other form of media, do you see all the intersecting roads of your identity represented?

Critical media literacy encourages us to look deeply into how representations are framed. This is important to gain a better understanding of both lack of diversity as well as complex presentations of diversity. Say you watch a movie where the main character represents a marginalized identity: Is the conflict centered around that identity component? When jokes are made, who (or what) are they directed at? **Framing**, by definition, includes and excludes certain components, telling the audience where (and how) they should direct their attention.

Conscious creators frame their content with various forms of imagery, word choice, and other conventions to convey a message. Chapter 7 will go into more detail about the techniques and effects of framing in corporate news media. For the purpose of this chapter, we discuss framing

in terms of entertainment media. How might the framing of media messages influence the way we make sense of real-world scenarios? What about our own identities?

Another way to assess how individuals and identities are represented in the media is through an analysis of **stereotypes**, as discussed in chapters 2 and 3, which are overgeneralized or fixed beliefs about a certain group. We can view the media as a powerful tool for producing or reproducing stereotypes and, therefore, shaping our beliefs beyond our lived experiences. As Lippmann explained, it can be difficult to change predetermined conceptions of a certain group, especially when we rely on understandings reinforced by the media. That is why it's important to identify and call attention to stereotypes in media content.

The Man Behind the Curtain

Another key approach to assessing representation is to look behind the scenes at ownership, production, and distribution. Media citizens understand that media content is consciously created: creators are real human beings with identities, values, and beliefs of their own, even though these aspects of the creators' identities may not be obvious in the content they create. In chapter 2 we discussed media ownership and the five companies that maintain control over much of what we do online. Of these powerful media corporations—Apple, Alphabet, Microsoft, Amazon, and

Meta—*all* have male CEOs. Three out of these five are white males. How might the individual identities of media creators influence what (or *whom*) we see in the media?

Media-literate citizens look behind the metaphoric curtain of media content to assess who constructs representations and what their underlying motivations or biases are. When we see depictions of historically underrepresented groups, we can ask ourselves, "Do the writers or producers have anything in common with the characters or content within the texts?" When those in charge of media production cannot thoroughly speak to an experience, identity, ability, and so on, media messages become susceptible to reflecting stereotypes and socially constructed representations. For example, in the early twentieth century, white producers created the "Sambo" caricature, which played on the prejudiced stereotype that Black people were lazy, docile, and content with servitude. This harmful depiction was an attempt to defend slavery and create the illusion (for white audiences) that slavery was beneficial to those it persecuted. What is the effect of white voices telling Black stories? How could this apply to other identities?

Who tells the story is just as important as the story itself. In the same way that producers make conscious choices in content creation, as media citizens we have the power to make choices about how we interpret, question, oppose or celebrate, and thus make meaning of the media we consume.

Representations of Race and Inequality

In the twenty-first century, race is understood as an ideological concept used to differentiate and categorize people based on real or imagined ethnic variances. Around the globe and throughout history, racial differences have been used to justify asserting dominance over others and to fuel racist beliefs based on presumed traits. Historically, "white" has been equated with racial superiority, constructed from baseless inferences of biological differences from other ethnicities. We see clear examples of this in early visual media, when racial stereotypes were blatant and direct.

Dated depictions of people of color in mainstream media openly used racist stereotypes. Blackface originated in vaudeville theater, where white actors would wear black makeup—making their faces "black"—to mock Black people, which was regarded as humorous and entertaining to white audiences at the time. When Black characters were finally allowed to play themselves in entertainment media, their roles were often exaggerations of hurtful racial stereotypes or they were shown as villains, servants, or sidekicks.

In the era of American enslavement (1619–1865), Northern white abolitionist newspapers and free Black periodicals produced markedly different representations of Black people, compared to other periodicals in either the North or the South. Frederick Douglass's *North Star* newspaper, produced in Rochester, New York—one of the last stops on the Underground Railroad—from 1847 to 1851, promoted free Black voices and published articles that condemned slavery as morally illegitimate. By contrast, Southern newspapers used the imagery of "happy darkies" to present an idyllic version of the slave South, while Northern newspapers with white readers acted as brokers for the buying and selling of slaves and even ran "wanted" advertisements for runaway enslaved persons. One scholarly study of these newspapers found that, from 1704 to 1807, Northern newspapers published more than 2,100 unique slave brokerage ads. These ads facilitated the buying and selling of up to 3,400 men, women, and children as chattel.[42]

From the very beginning, race, racial oppression, and anti-Blackness were fundamental to the very business operation of American newspaper media, even in the so-called free Northern states. That legacy would, of course, continue in the post-slavery era and necessitate the rise of Black newspapers that were directly responsible to their communities and which amplified Black community voices to represent events ignored or distorted by white-owned media across the United States. Black-owned papers such as the *New York Amsterdam News*, the *Chicago Defender*, the *Pittsburgh Courier*, and the *Oakland Post* represented a response to the white-owned news media's deliberate racial misrepresentations.

Overt racism is less common in contemporary media, but that is not to say that the unequal treatment and representation of people of color is only a matter of history.

Today's nonfiction and news media predominantly feature negative stories or portrayals of people of color. Black people are often denied roles on screen and off screen in the entertainment industry. Implicit racism, which indirectly draws on harmful stereotypes, appears in the portrayal in film of Black characters as criminals or villains.

We can see the role of intersectionality in representations of race in the media as well. Black women, Black people in the LGBTQIA+ community, and other people of color intersecting with marginalized identities suffer disproportionately in their representation in the media. For example, women of color are less likely to be directors and writers for television shows compared to their white, female counterparts.[43]

When women of color do achieve prominence as star celebrities, the power of the connections between race and media are often complex. Consider the case of the artist Nicki Minaj, often cited as the "queen of hip hop." In September 2021, Minaj tweeted that she would not be attending the 2021 Met Gala because of its COVID-19 vaccine requirement, and that she would get vaccinated only after she felt she had "done enough research." In a subsequent tweet, she related how a cousin of hers in Trinidad refused to get vaccinated because a friend of his "became impotent" after receiving the vaccine. Minaj concluded this tweet by noting "make sure you're comfortable with ur decision, not bullied."[44]

Every major American news outlet amplified Minaj's

tweets. Many pointed out that there was no scientific evidence linking COVID-19 vaccines with fertility problems in men or women. But even in the process of debunking misinformation in Minaj's tweet, news coverage of Minaj's tweets became a prominent part of the public debate on COVID-19 vaccines.

Why was Minaj's tweet elevated to a national story? What authority did Minaj carry on COVID-19 and vaccines? Why did some news outlets choose to prop Minaj up as a voice representing all Black people? We can make sense of the coverage by recalling the concept of interpretive communities, introduced in chapter 1. Minaj was presented to Black media consumers based on stereotypical assumptions about her relevance as an important public figure in Black communities; she was presented to white and other non-Black audiences for entertainment purposes—on one level as a kind of modern-day minstrel, and on another level as an example of the depths of Black ignorance regarding the COVID-19 pandemic.

Neither representation served the medical needs of the Black community. The amplification of Minaj's tweet did nothing to protect the lives of any American, whatever their ethnic or racial identification. Instead, the reporting of Minaj's tweet tied to a web of broader, politically motivated conspiracy thinking regarding the vaccine. For instance, the Fox News host Tucker Carlson picked up on the story, championing Minaj's public tweets as a new way to raise doubts about the safety and effectiveness of COVID-19 vaccines.[45] Carlson's amplification of Minaj's Twitter messages did nothing to help save lives in Black communities in the midst of a global pandemic. Through the lens of critical media literacy, we can see how the subsequent news coverage of Nicki Minaj's tweet functioned as "clickbait" designed to appeal in distinct ways to different interpretive communities, but not necessarily to inform any of them. (The section on algorithmic literacy in chapter 5 digs deeper into how media amplified Minaj's tweet.)

For now, though, we can note that, although media have come a long way from their explicit racism in representations of Black people in particular, and of people of color more generally, in important ways the old prejudices remain intact. As long as there are race-based inequalities in our society, the media are likely to reflect—and to reproduce—those inequalities. Calling attention to misrepresentations is one way to begin healing from them and putting them behind us.

Constructions of Gender and Sexuality

The social constructs that we see in the media often reinforce outdated portrayals of gender and narrow depictions of sexuality. Our society has historically "normalized" gender to fit into a male-female gender binary. But some people do not identify with their sex assigned at birth, and some do not align with a gender at all! Society has only recently begun to recognize, and represent, a more complex and flexible understanding of gender. Similarly, we can look at how society has constructed heterosexuality as the norm for acceptance. Again, this is a very narrow depiction of reality. The ever-evolving LGBTQIA+ community encompasses a broad range of sexualities and identities, stepping away from the notion that there is any single "right" way to express love or identify according to gender.

So how does the media play into all of this? We have learned that media creators consciously choose who characters are and how they are depicted. Media producers may try in good faith to work around limiting representations. For example, during the time of the Hays Code (1934–1968), when homosexual characters were barred from appearing in film, creators adopted coded ways of depicting LGBTQIA+ people on screen. But this inclusion was not necessarily a positive development: many times, these characters were cast as sexual criminals or quirky sidekicks, often exhibiting stereotypical traits of flamboyance or promiscuity.

Nowadays, we can see LGBTQIA+ bodies as some of our favorite characters, but their representation is still conditional. Oftentimes, their sexuality or gender identity, if straying from the "norm," is framed as a struggle or conflict to overcome. For example, the "coming out" narrative uses queerness as a central theme of contention, where a character will inevitably face backlash for this component of their identity. One question we may ask of our media is, "When will LGBTQIA+ characters just 'be'?" That is, when will their coming out not have to serve as a main plot point, but instead be represented as a seamless part of their lives? Furthermore, gay men encompass the majority of LGBTQIA+ visibility, which presents a narrow depiction of the intersectionality of identities among queer people.[46]

Characters who are not white, male, or **cisgender** are often mistreated or even ignored in the media. Women are more regularly seen than other marginalized genders, but their depiction has historically reinforced harmful gender roles and stereotypes: media have subtly reinforced the view that women are submissive, sexual, domestic humans by placing women in roles that objectify their bodies or by creating characters that strive to be mothers and are often depicted as inferiors to their male counterparts. Women are disproportionately excluded from roles behind the scenes of entertainment media as well.[47] For example, while we are used to seeing women on screen (and we may be able to name many women actors and influencers), it may be harder to name women writers, producers, and directors. Therefore, even when women are portrayed as powerful on-screen, we also want to dig deeper behind the screens to see who created and developed those characters.

Linguistic Representation, Profiling, and Stereotyping in Film and TV

Linguistic representation is the way that different languages, dialects, accents, and speech patterns are presented or omitted in mainstream media. Different ways of spoken and signed communication can be a result of which language(s) a person knows, where they live or were raised, their cultural backgrounds, socioeconomic status, and neurological and motor capabilities. Just like other aspects of identity, media utilize linguistic identity to create a picture of a character based on inferences that come from widely held stereotypes.[48]

Although it makes sense to include certain languages, accents, and dialects in certain settings, the omission of these can lead to an inaccurate representation of an actual place, culture, or ethnic group. Take Disney's 1992 animated film *Aladdin*. The Disney story is based on the Arabic folktale "Aladdin" from the Middle Eastern folk collection *One Thousand and One Nights*. The movie takes place in the fictional city of Agrabah, which is understood to be somewhere in the Middle East. Despite the story's setting and cultural backdrop, the movie was originally written and recorded in English. We might infer from this that the original target audience for this movie was English-speaking American and European families. What is curious about the linguistic representations in this movie is the fact that the main characters all have Anglo-American accents while secondary and background characters who are portrayed as greedy or villainous have heavy Arabic accents; this choice of linguistic representation sends a message that people with foreign accents are "bad."

Assuming character traits based on language use and accent is called **linguistic stereotyping**. Attempting to identify an aspect of an individual's identity solely on the basis of how they speak or write is called **linguistic profiling**. Factors that play into linguistic profiling may include intonation (the rise and fall of the voice in speaking), pitch (high, medium, or low/deep), timing (quick or slow), and voice quality (breathy, modal, or creaky). Some movies and shows capitalize on these aspects of speech to drive home a certain aspect of a character's identity, such as their race, gender expression and identity, or sexual orientation. This attempt at identification of identity based on voice can quickly slip into linguistic stereotyping, which leads to assumptions of how someone may act or the views they might hold. However, identity is complex and an individual's voice does not necessarily correspond with ethnic, racial, sexual, or gender identities, nor does it indicate their moral values or other characteristics.

One possible way to avoid this issue of linguistic profiling and stereotyping in films is to hire actors who are native speakers of the language used in the setting of the story and then use subtitles to make the media accessible in other languages. Alternatively, a studio could hire actors who are native speakers of the target audience's language, and then have those actors utilize the accent of the language they would logically be speaking in the movie's time and setting. Having linguistic representation accurately reflect the linguistic identities featured in a film's setting can help lessen the chances of linguistic profiling and stereotyping.

Going back to the *Aladdin* example, it is worth noting that Disney+ has provided dubbing and subtitles in multiple languages for the animated film. Yet languages commonly spoken in the Middle East, such as Arabic, Persian, Turkish, Kurdish, Hebrew, and Greek, are not supported. Logically, all the characters in this movie would be speaking Arabic, or at the very least, they would speak English with a non-Anglo-American accent. How far to go toward the usage of a certain linguistic trait such as an accent or dialect is a question worth asking. What can be considered appropriate for the setting, and what could take the trait usage too far, thus creating linguistic or ethnic stereotypes?

Clearly, movies and other visual media can use linguistic identities to convey to the audience implicit background on characters' identities. As media citizens, it is important to be cognizant of how media can use linguistic stereotyping and profiling and ultimately create or reinforce audience members' beliefs and biases.

Advertisements also use language, dialect, and accent to appeal to different audiences. The use of bilingual and

Considering Language and Movies

Think about your favorite movie. What is it called? Who were the main characters and who are the actors who portrayed them? After answering these questions, consider the following:.

◘ Where is the movie set? (What country or land does the action take place in?)

◘ What cultures are depicted in the movie?

◘ What language was the original audio for the movie recorded in?

◘ Do the accents or dialects of the characters in the movie fit the setting or cultures?

◘ Do the actors speak the same language or dialect, or with the same accent as the characters?

◘ Based on what you've discovered, which linguistic identities does the movie's target audience have?

◘ How do you think the messages end up taking so much space online?

multilingual advertisements on mainstream television has increased over time to appeal to wider linguistic demographics.

In contrast to companies utilizing different linguistic representations in their commercials, nation-wide TV news organizations tend to omit accents and dialects from their broadcasts. Have you ever noticed that many news anchors sound similar to each other? This is because these anchors speak with what linguists call "general" or "standard" American accents. Although there really is no "standard" form of English, this accent has been dubbed as such because it is composed of many North American accents. This accent, which has come to be regarded as lacking any distinctive qualities of regional, socioeconomic, or ethnic characteristics, is also referred to as "Broadcast English" because it is the one most commonly adopted by news anchors. Just as with other forms of media, these choices in linguistic representation are made to appeal to a wide audience.

Although there is no way to speak without any accent or dialect, it is important to become aware of how media content invokes linguistic identities, and the implications of these representations.

Representations of Family and Class

When we discuss class in the United States, we are referring to the categorization of people based on their economic status. In mainstream media, most characters do not discuss their class, but if they do, this aspect of their identity is typically central to the narrative, either in terms of exhibiting extreme wealth or of overcoming poverty.

We can circle back to our understanding of ownership and production as driving forces behind media representations of class and its importance. Because most mass media are for-profit businesses, advertisers are keenly aware of the perceived class of their audiences. Advertisers seek audiences with disposable income. Class is not just important for on-screen representation; the class of the consumer is equally important to media producers. (Chapter 6 goes into deeper detail about the role of advertising in media.)

In television, we often see families represented as wealthier than they would be in real life. Characters may be professionally employed—think about how many TV shows are about doctors, lawyers, and businesspeople—but the source of our entertainment does not come from watching them work. A limited number of television programs depict working-class families, but their struggles are often framed for comedic value or their economic status is framed for dramatic effect. Representations never "slip" too far down the class ladder; instead, characters usually range from middle-class to wealthy.

Television has consistently struggled to embrace diverse representations of families in their content, beyond class status. TV has shown us over the years that the "normal" family is white and middle-class, and that they live in the suburbs, with multiple children and monogamous heterosexual parents. This is one of those social constructs we have discussed throughout this text: a generalized depiction of family that society has evolved to regard as the "norm." As in our other discussions of identity components, this type of representation is not actually exemplary of the diversity and variations of family structure that exist in real life. Many viewers know that their own family does not look anything like the "normal" families shown on television; in real life, familial conflict is not solved in a twenty-five-minute season finale, our family is not always blood-related, and there may not always be a happy ending.

Assessing Ability

In the United States, about 26 percent of the population has some type of physical or neurological disability, according to the Centers for Disease Control and Prevention, yet in primetime television, just 3.5 percent of recurring characters have such disabilities.[49] Once again, we sound the alarm that mainstream media offer a limited, misleading representation of reality.

When we are presented with a character that is not able-bodied or neurotypical, they are often framed in a way that invalidates or distorts the everyday reality for people with some type of disability. Over the years, media have shown characters with disabilities as sad, in need of "fixing," or as a stable sidekick for an able-bodied counterpart. Many times, these roles are played by able-bodied or neurotypical actors. Similar to our discussion of gender and sexuality in the media, those who stray from the norm are often played by actors that identify with traditionally "acceptable" traits in terms of class, race, and gender—usually wealthy white

Who Tells Your Story?

Imagine you are going to produce a movie about your life. Answer these questions and ask yourself, "How do I want my story to be told?"

◘ Who is writing your screenplay? Who will direct the movie?

◘ Who will you cast to play the role of *you*?

◘ What type of movie will it be? A comedy? A horror film?

◘ What pieces of your identity and experience will you add to the plot?

men. In other words, the lack of alignment between the identity of a character and that of its actor means that they act out a narrative that is not their story to tell.

It is important to acknowledge that some media have been successful in representing characters with disabilities in a way that counters harmful, unjustified stereotypes. The television series *Special* tells the intersectional story of a gay man with cerebral palsy, who is played by an actor of corresponding disability and sexual orientation. Here we can refer back to the understanding that to be critical of media is not to be negative. Instead, we can assess examples of representation and recognize their successes while at the same time acknowledging inequalities that continue to exist.

Representations Reveal Literacies

There really is nothing easy about representation. Even though all our media are doing the work of representing, it is still very difficult to parse the meaningful bits and pieces and to distinguish between what was built into the text and how we interpret it. As you have read, it can be especially challenging to make representations in the media as complex and complicated as they may be in our own lived experience. Our media cannot tackle everything about who we are as individuals, but they do give us an opportunity to see how parts of ourselves are shared (or ignored). Just as we have multiple aspects to our identity that intersect to create a unified whole, there are multiple components to the analysis of media representations of identity.

CHAPTER 5

Multiple Literacies

Expanding the Idea of "Literacy"

When asked to envision a TikTok trend, you probably would not think of a scientist reading graphs and analyzing data. However, that is what happened in 2021, when Dr. Anna Blakney, a professor at the University of British Columbia whose research focuses on biomedical engineering, made a series of TikTok videos that went viral. Blakney's videos aimed to teach people about the science behind COVID-19 vaccines. They were meant to convince vaccine-hesitant people that these vaccines' scientific design and testing could be trusted. "It may seem like a silly idea but it's actually turned out to be a powerful way to show people what I do in the lab and answer any questions they may have about vaccines," explained Blakney.[50]

A March 2021 story in Vancouver Is Awesome, an online news site, referred to Blakney's videos as "hilarious vaccine literacy videos."[51] On Earth Day in April 2021, the editorial board of the *Mercury News* urged people to "promote greater scientific literacy." The editorial lauded President Joe Biden's ambitious goals for combating climate change, but worried that if the public was not "literate" in the subject of science that they would not understand the proposal's significance and urgency, or ways to participate in it.[52] Both Anna Blakney's and the *Mercury News*'s uses of the word "literacy"—vaccine literacy and scientific literacy—expand the narrow, traditional definition of literacy.

Literacy is so much more than the ability to read and write. The National Literacy Trust explains that literacy is "the ability to read, write, speak and listen in a way that lets us communicate effectively and make sense of the world."[53] Indeed, literacy involves not only reading books, articles, and essays, but also consuming diverse forms of new and old media, including films, songs, programs, posters, and paintings. Robust literacy enables the user to interpret and communicate independently. Given the wide variety of media, critical media literacy is grounded in the idea of *multiple* literacies. Being a media citizen means being multi-literate. This chapter deepens our understanding of multiple literacies by defining and discussing visual, aural, and digital literacy.

Ways of Communicating

In our increasingly connected and digitized world, we continue to witness the development of new forms of communication. Whenever we wish to speak with someone else, we can choose from a wide array of media-based communication, including (but not limited to) text messaging, direct or instant messaging through an app, phone calls, emailing, video chatting over FaceTime or Zoom, tagging our friends in social media posts, and **subtweeting** (the practice of directing a post toward someone without tagging them or sending it directly to them). In most of these options, we can choose to communicate through a written message, a voice message, a picture, or a video. Much as in face-to-face conversation, media-based communication leaves room for misinterpretation.

Can you recall a time there might have been a misunderstanding between you and someone else? Maybe this happened when you were texting a friend and they misunderstood the intent of your text. Maybe you have felt this way when the person you like messaged you "hey." There could be many different ways to interpret this message. Did they text it to you through your phone's messaging app? Through Snapchat or Instagram DMs? When they texted you first last time, did they also put only one *y* at the end? Maybe they put exclamation marks at the end of it, or perhaps a question mark or period. Do any of these different factors change the way you might interpret this one-word message?

As it turns out, professionals have researched this and have found that there are many different ways that people might understand this simple one-word text message. Your interpretation of "hey" could change based on how the sender spelled the word, what messaging *medium* they sent it through, and what punctuation they used. The George-

Thinking about Texts and Metamessaging

Think about the most recent text message you've sent. Who was it to? What medium did you send your message over? What did the message say? After answering these questions, consider the following:

◘ Do you think your message would have been interpreted differently if you had sent it through a different medium, such as an email or a voice message?

◘ Would you have worded your message differently if you were sending it to a different person?

◘ Do you think that your message would have been interpreted differently if you used different punctuation and included (or left out) emojis?

town University linguistics professor Deborah Tannen has studied the different ways that people communicate with each other and how their selection of medium can influence others' understanding of what they say. It's not just *what* you say or message to someone but *how* you say or message it that affects how others interpret it. Tannen calls this **metamessaging**.[54]

Metamessaging is a form of **paralinguistic communication**, which is a means of conveying meaning in dialogue outside the words themselves. In face-to-face communication, this could look like an eye-roll, a sigh, a smile, or a laugh. (Remember the blinks and winks we discussed in the introduction?) In media-based communication, paralinguistic communication could include the use of multiple exclamation points, all capital letters, emojis or emoticons, or the choice of medium for sending the message. A text message that reads "hey" can be interpreted differently than a DM or IM that says "hey!!!" or an email that opens with "hello." Awareness of metamessaging can help you better tailor your response to the person with whom you are communicating. Being able to interpret someone's intended meaning from a message is a form of literacy.

Visual Literacy
Visual representations such as memes, films, pictures, and drawings communicate meaning. Understanding this

process is known as **visual literacy**, which is the ability to analyze, interpret, and negotiate the meanings of imagery in TV, movies, gaming, and news. Just as a media producer can choose the message they seek to communicate, the user has the ability to interpret the messages. For example, the "OK" hand sign—where an individual connects their index and thumb into a circle while raising their remaining fingers—has historically communicated approval, but has more recently been adopted by the Proud Boys, a far-right, neo-fascist organization, as a symbol of white supremacy. This is one example of how some of us might attach meaning to visual symbols that may differ from the meaning that other people attach to those symbols. An "OK" hand sign could indicate approval to one person and white supremacy to another.

The production of visual images involves decisions about what to depict and how to arrange the subject matter in space. For example, a portrait of a person, focused closely on their face, can encourage you to see them as a unique individual, with personal characteristics and feelings. By contrast, a photograph of a group of people, taken at some distance from them, may lead you to see those people as a "crowd," rather than as individuals.

These may seem like very simple matters, and it might seem as though some messages are "just that way." But we invite you to consider that any visual image can be carefully constructed as a way to communicate some message. This

means asking deeper questions about who made the visual: Why did they create it? What is its intended meaning? What do the producers' choices regarding representation reveal about the visual?

Digital platforms and software have allowed users to capture, edit, and share video at a level of quality and speed that was available only to Hollywood just a generation ago. The use of video has helped mobilize powerful movements such as Black Lives Matter (BLM). Videos distributed online have been crucial to BLM garnering national and international support. For example, the video of George Floyd's murder drove millions of people, who had never met Floyd or visited his community, to take to the streets and demand justice. This is a testament to the power of visual media. However, that power can be also used to manipulate users.

Photographs Are Persuasive Communication Tools

Many people take photographs and share them on social media. Digital tools and platforms allow users to edit these pictures in a variety of ways, such as by changing the photograph's color tone or reframing its object of focus. Those are decisions meant to communicate specific messages to the image's viewers.

Look at the front page of different national news outlets, ideally ones that are from different political positions (such as the *New York Times* and the *Wall Street Journal*). You can start by visiting the (digital) front pages of online news outlets that appear on your social media feed. (Newseum's online feature

"Today's Front Pages" is also a great resource for this purpose.[130])

◪ Are the front-page images similar or different? How so?

◪ How does each news source alter or frame the news photographs featured on the front page?

◪ Take a look at your town's local newspaper; what images are featured on its front page? How does your town's notion of the top story correspond with the top story in the national news?

◪ Consider the relationship between these news photographs and the captions that accompanies them. How does each caption shape your interpretation of the photograph? And how does the photograph relate to the caption?

Rather than accept the old adage that "'seeing is believing," critical media literacy recognizes that like any other media, visual media can be manipulated to mislead and misinform users. This problem has grown more complicated with the development of machine learning and artificial intelligence, which make possible the production of fraudulent videos, known as **deep fakes**. Deep fakes appear real, but are in fact synthetic media, where the image of one person is blended with or replaced by another in such a way that the alteration is invisible to the image's viewers.[55] For example, in 2020 a deep fake video surfaced that portrayed the speaker of the House of Representatives, Nancy Pelosi, appearing to slur her words and speak incoherently, as if she were drunk. The video was fake. Pelosi was not drunk, nor was her speech incoherent, but technology allowed the video's creator to create this false impression of Pelosi. In this case, the poor quality of the video resulted in ire and laughter from audiences, who did not fall for the trick. However, when deep fake technology has allowed users to put the faces of real humans—such as celebrities, colleagues, and people in their inner circle—on other people's bodies in videos, the result is not always a laughing matter. In some cases, deep fakes have destroyed people's reputations and livelihoods.

Aural Literacy

During his terms as president of the United States (1933–1945), Franklin Roosevelt frequently gave speeches on the radio that he referred to as "fireside chats." In these talks, he spoke directly to the American public as if he were sitting in front of a fireplace in a living room with them. He used this as an opportunity to bypass journalists and to speak directly to Americans, in an effort to mobilize their support for his rather ambitious agenda. Roosevelt's "fireside chats" were such a powerful tool that the imagery associated with them is still remembered today.

However, in reality, Roosevelt was not sitting next to a fireplace. This was a powerful auditory tool for shaping audience interpretations. All audio is constructed to convey a message. Think of podcasts: the number of hosts or the use of background sound can change how you interpret the podcast's meaning. Aurally literate media users employ their critical-listening skills to ask deeper questions about the process of production: What is the intended meaning of the content? What tools of representation are used in it? These questions are at the heart of aural literacy.

Aural literacy refers to the ability to analyze, interpret, and negotiate the meaning of sound. Auditory media can shape audience interpretations as much as any other type of media. For example, have you ever listened to a song in a language that you do not understand and still had a sense of whether it expressed joy or sadness? Not only do critical media listeners accept their initial interpretation of the audio, they dig deeper into the message, process, representations, and more. For example, musicians have long used fast or upbeat music to mask darker messages. Think about your favorite (or least favorite) song: What do the lyrics *mean*? Does the music match the lyrics? What feeling do you get from that song? Aurally literate audiences can negotiate meaning by comparing the intended meaning of the song with their interpretation.

Just as a song's beat can add a feeling that is different from the feeling conveyed by its lyrics alone, sound effects shape our understanding of content. For example, television and radio have long used laugh tracks to cue audiences to what they are supposed to interpret as funny and when they are supposed to laugh. Similarly, film relies on sound effects. Think of the jarring, high-pitched sound you might have heard accompanied by a dark screen. Chances are, this is from a horror film, and the uncomfortable sound coupled with the feeling of being unable to see anything prompts fearful emotions in viewers. (Try watching a

Songs Are an Influential Instrument of Communication

What is the most recent song you listened to? As you listen to it again, consider the following questions:

◘ What unexpected emotions, memories, or sensory experiences surfaced while listening to the song?

◘ What idea is the artist concerned about?

◘ Does the song make you aware of something you did not know before?

◘ How do the lyrics relate to the tempo or beat of the song?

horror film with the sound *off*—it becomes much less scary!) Video games are no different, relying on faster music to provide a sense of intensity or importance to something transpiring in the game. Finally, podcasters use added sounds for specific effect—for example, crunching leaves to demonstrate that they are walking in a wooded area. Podcasters can also make the audience feel the distance between the program's hosts if they muffle and drop the audio on one person's voice to make them sound further away. This provides the illusion that the audience and host are closer and everyone else is distant. These uses of sound illustrate how audio can shape our sense of a media message.

Digital and Algorithmic Literacy

At the start of the digital information age, many people hoped that the internet would create a more democratic world by removing barriers to accessing and sharing information. The internet, and especially social media platforms, have increased access to information, allowed for groups of people with shared interests or identities to connect, and opened up instantaneous communication channels among people across the world. Nonetheless, as with other technologies, the internet is not neutral.

The same platforms that allow for the creation and organization of social movements such as Black Lives Matter, also provide a space for some virulent groups to spread hate, propaganda, misinformation, and disinformation. Although misinformation, disinformation, and propaganda are nothing new, the way the internet and social media multiply the power of individuals and groups to reach a global audience is cause for concern. Before the internet, traditional media served as a sort of gatekeeper, selecting what messages were circulated and which were suppressed, who and what was published, and what books appeared in stores and libraries. With the openness of the internet and the speed and scope of online information, users need to develop their digital literacy skills to prepare for countering or dealing with disinformation, propaganda, and misinformation.

Digital literacy may be understood as a variant of media literacy with a specific focus on digital media and the internet. Digital literacy has two aspects. First, functional literacy includes the practical skills and knowledge necessary to use the internet and engage with others online. But the ability to use the internet or to communicate with others through social media is not all that matters.

A second aspect of digital literacy includes thinking critically about socioeconomic issues that affect how information is produced, accessed, and used in a digital age. Critical digital literacy includes consideration of how advertising and ownership shape the production and consumption of online content, the relationships between content creators and consumers, and the consequences of these.

For example, consider a 2021 report about new research on the hidden rules of advertising technology and how these affect news coverage of humanitarian crises, such as famine. Advertisers now use "blocklists" to avoid having their products associated with content that they believe might damage their brands' reputations in the eyes of consumers. Some of these restrictions make good sense and probably represent widely shared values: no advertiser wants their product associated with child pornography or terrorism, for example. But as research shows, the advertising blocklists used by many prominent corporations now employ advertising technology to scan for as many as seven thousand different words and phrases in the name of "brand safety." Many advertising blocklists now include terms such as "conflict" or "famine" or phrases that identify racial groups, sexual orientations, or religion.[56] Even though the credit company Mastercard and its Mastercard Foundation Scholars Program for refugees partner with the United Nations refugee agency, the UNHCR, Mastercard's December 2020 advertising blocklist included the word "refugees."[57] As a result, no Mastercard advertising would appear next to any news report that included the blocked term.

These advertising blocklists have at least two related and significant negative impacts for news reporting on humanitarian crises. First, as Kate Wright, an expert in media and communication at the University of Edinburgh, explains, excessive automatic ad blocking "deprives the news organizations which report on humanitarian issues of much-needed income."[58] (See chapter 6 for more on the relationship between advertising interests and media content.) Second, reductions in advertising revenues driven by blocklists may ultimately cause news publishers to reduce their coverage of humanitarian crises. As Ben Parker reported for The New Humanitarian, "Hard news about humanitarian and social issues is being treated as toxic by overzealous ad technology, undermining corporate social responsibility and effectively punishing publishers for reporting on international crises."[59]

Advertising blocklists operate "backstage" and so are nearly invisible to most of us when we read the news or use other forms of media. Critical digital literacy is about expanding our awareness to include what's not always obvious, equipping ourselves with the skills to make informed choices online. It's about ensuring that everyone has the basic digital skills to understand simple facts about services that have become part of daily life, such as how search engines rank the results they provide, why a social media platform shows some news stories but not others, and why many "free" online services charge no money but make use of peoples' personal data in tricky ways.[60]

The User Is the Product

Although many of us enjoy free-to-use platforms such as TikTok, Snapchat, Facebook, Twitter, Instagram, and many others, we should also be aware that these are commercial providers, with profit-making intentions, which may not (and often do not) have our best interests in mind. Research shows that "the majority of internet users are unaware that a search engine or a social network is free to use because advertisers pay the platforms to show consumers their advertisements" and that the user is the product.[61] Anytime we are online, interacting with these services, these platforms are monitoring our behaviors in order to "harvest" useful information about us.

As you navigate any digital environment, whether it is Google's search engine or social media platforms such as Snapchat, TikTok, or Instagram, each of your actions is a data point. The information you search for, the comments you make, your IP address, your location while browsing, and so forth are all collected by web browsers, survey forms you may choose to complete, comments you post, as well as information (both public and private) that you share on social media platforms, and GPS data from your smart phone. Tech companies collect a seemingly endless stream of data from cell phones, smart televisions and remotes, in-home assistants such as Amazon's Alexa, facial-recognition security cameras, DNA samples from ancestry websites, video calls such as Zoom, and educational soft-

ware and platforms.[62] There is no "time out" when it comes to data collection. These companies are listening and watching *all the time*. They use techniques designed to keep users on their screen because more screen time means more data for their use. To maximize their data collection, these companies also share their data with each other.[63] In turn, this data is fed back into algorithms that determine the content you see online, further shaping and individualizing your experience.

At its most basic sense, an **algorithm** is a designed process or set of rules. Computer programmers use coding as a form of language to provide these algorithms with instruction for analyzing data. Algorithms themselves are not inherently good or bad; instead, their effects ultimately depend on what they are programmed to do, who is doing the programming, how users interact with them, and what companies such as Google and Facebook then do with the huge amount of personal data they collect.

Digital tech companies are businesses that pursue profits in service to their shareholders. These corporations are some of the most valuable stocks in the US market, collectively worth $2.9 trillion. But how much do you know about these companies' histories, business models, and values? You might have watched videos or read online to learn how to make your own content trend or how to monetize it, but it's also important to explore how these companies actually make their money. We can start by taking a look at the capital streams of Meta (which owns Facebook, Instagram, and Oculus) and Alphabet (which owns Google and YouTube). More than 97 percent of Meta's revenue comes from advertisements and more than 88 percent of Alphabet's wealth comes from Google AdWords and YouTube. Those are big numbers, but how do they matter for you?

To create consumer markets, algorithms forge through users' profile data and analyze the information for self-identified interests, traits, correlations, and preferences that group users into a sort of caste, the term used to describe how status is determined by a person's background. You might think, "Good, so the content in my feed is tailored to my own interests? What's so bad about that?"

By using algorithms that rank and organize content in

search engine results and social media feeds, tech companies filter out content that is likely to reduce users' engagement on the platform.[64] A first and fairly obvious problem arises from the possibility that you may be interested in ("engaged by") content that is unpopular, because most other people see it as dull, offensive, or simply "not engaging." Because of how the algorithms that organize online searches and social media feeds work, you will have to be much more proactive in finding the kind of content that interests you. "So what?" you might respond, "I like a good challenge and I'm pretty sharp when it comes to web searches."

A deeper, more insidious problem involves how the content promoted by online algorithms privileges appeals to human emotions. These appeals invoke positive emotions—such as admiration, appreciation, amusement, love, satisfaction, sympathy, and triumph—and negative ones—such as anxiety, awkwardness, boredom, confusion, craving, disgust, envy, fear, horror, and sadness—because emotions are "hooks" that hold our online attention and engagement most firmly.[65]

But online content seldom balances positive and negative emotions; instead, the overwhelming emphasis online is on doubt, uncertainty, and fear. The Propwatch Project, a nonprofit educational website focused on raising public awareness about "the prevalence of propaganda and disinformation in mass media," shows how media techniques designed to heighten anxiety or raise doubt also "make it hard to think rationally and easier to draw conclusions that might be counter to logic or common sense."[66] Media messages that promote demonizing—defined on the Propwatch website as "characterizing a group or those who support an opposing viewpoint as threatening, immoral, or less than human"—and scapegoating—"placing unmerited blame on a person or group to channel societal resentment and frustration towards a common adversary or powerless victim"—are obvious examples. But the Propwatch Project also shows how less overt techniques, such as dog whistles—"ambiguous messaging used to stoke racial fear and anxiety and/or to covertly signal allegiance to certain subgroups of an audience"—and FUDs—"making dire warnings or raising doubt about an issue," while providing "little or no specifics or evidence to support the claims"— aim to disarm our critical-thinking skills and appeal to our negative emotions. Beyond our introduction of several common emotion-triggering techniques, the Propwatch Project maintains a rich archive of actual, contemporary examples of these techniques at work. (Not impressed yet? In keeping with its commitment to nonpartisanship, the Propwatch Project examines all this content using the same standards, so that evidence—rather than partisan politics— informs their analyses.)

From Prediction to Direction: The "Action" Economy

Returning to our focus on digital literacy, some media critics argue that algorithmic-driven content has led to an **action economy**. The purpose of all this data and analysis is not only to understand users' behaviors and attitudes but also to actively manipulate them.[67] In other words, corporations use customers' data to *direct* rather than *predict* those customers' behavior. Data offers a window into users' thoughts and cognitive processes. The goal is to capture your attention long enough for you to click hyperlinks (which reveal more information about what interests you) or, better yet, to purchase a product. Your attention and engagement are interpreted as validation. This empowers the algorithm to continue to feed you similar content with limited accountability—no matter how problematic the content—because the platform's profitability depends on collecting and analyzing data derived from prolonged media use.

Marketing insiders claim that the insights provided by data analysis enable them to anticipate a user's response or behavior.[68] These are known as **predictive analytic products**. These data-driven predictions help both profit-seeking companies and vote-seeking political parties to microtarget effective messages to specific individuals or groups. The effectiveness of these messages is enhanced by the reality that most of the people subject to these techniques are unaware of being targeted.

Predictive analytic products serve different functions for various industries: health insurers would like to know what ailments their patients have searched for on Google and how physically active they are in order to calculate their patients' health insurance fees; car insurance companies seek Global Positioning System (GPS) data to analyze their customers' driving speed and frequency in order to calculate insurance premiums; law enforcement agencies seek DNA data from genealogy websites in order to solve crimes; and advertisers seek customer data to create effective advertisements.[69] At present, none of these practices are subject to rigorous government regulation.

Because algorithms sometimes use limited or biased datasets to predict outcomes, they may produce bad results, such as when a student gets accepted into college on the basis of their zip code and not just their academic merit.[70] In other cases, the emphasis that admissions algorithms place on certain types of data may perpetuate preexisting inequalities. For instance, a September 2021 report from the Brookings Institution (a public policy think tank that has been described as politically liberal or centrist) reported that colleges' use of algorithms to inform admissions decisions generally reduces "the amount of scholarship funding offered to students."[71] Because the algorithms that colleges use to inform their admissions decisions are very good at identifying a student's ability to pay tuition, these algorithms can "drive enrollment while also reducing students' chances to persist and graduate."[72] In sum, algorithms may worsen the crises of low graduation rates, high student debt, and "stagnant inequality for racial minorities" in higher education, according to the Brookings study.

This imbalance of power and knowledge may also be used in attempts to influence our political attitudes and voting decisions. During the 2016 presidential election, Cambridge Analytica, a political consulting firm based in the United Kingdom, helped Donald Trump's campaign gather and analyze vast amounts of user data from Facebook in an effort to influence the results of the presidential election in Trump's favor. Journalists working for the *Guardian*, in the United Kingdom, and the *New York Times*, in the United States, were the first to report this story, based on information provided by a **whistleblower**, who revealed how Cambridge Analytica helped the Trump campaign target American voters.[73]

Combining personal data gathered from millions of Facebook users with some basic (if cynical) models of human psychology, Cambridge Analytica created a system that exploited the private social media activity of those Facebook users to target them with personalized political advertisements. Only a "tiny fraction" of these users had agreed to have their data shared with a third party, the *New York Times* later reported.[74]

Cambridge Analytica used this information to manipulate US voters.[75] The aim was to swing the presidential election in Trump's favor. To this end, Cambridge Analytica and the Trump campaign developed political advertisements that would appeal to individuals' demographic and psychological profiles. There is much more that could be said about the Facebook-Cambridge Analytica data scandal, but there are two basic takeaways. First, using algorithms, Cambridge Analytica analyzed private information from the Facebook profiles of millions of users. This information had been gathered without those users' permissions, making this one of the "largest data leaks" in Facebook's history.[76] Second, Cambridge Analytica and the Trump campaign used this data to influence the opinions of voters in deciding the outcome of a presidential election. Subsequent investigations have demonstrated that, in addition to the 2016 US presidential election, Cambridge Analytica partnered with politicians and political parties in other countries to influence election results.

Filter Bubbles and Content Moderation

The power of algorithms to influence the media content we see—and thus to potentially influence what we believe and even how we choose to act—contributes to the creation of filter bubbles. A **filter bubble** is an environment, especially online, in which people are exposed only to opinions and information that conform to their existing beliefs. Filter bubbles discourage diverse opinions and perspectives from penetrating your digital sphere. Platforms maximize the time users spend on their sites by employing recommender algorithms that feed us information that we are likely to agree with, and by automatically filtering out content we might disagree with. Because these systems work "behind the scenes," we are usually unaware of the content that we cannot see. Once this individualized experience is created, it is difficult to break free from the patterns established by the platform's (hidden) recommender system, especially if we are not aware of how algorithms work. Recall, for example, how Cambridge Analytica exploited the private data of millions of Facebook users in an attempt to help Donald Trump win the 2016 presidential election. In effect, the targeted political ads produced by Cambridge Analytica and the Trump campaign sought to reinforce the beliefs of Trump's supporters by appealing to their preexisting concerns and fears.

Filter bubbles amplify the in-group–out-group dynamics that we examined in chapter 1. On an individual level, personalization of information flows and the resulting filter bubbles may lead to reassurance and the reinforcement of our individual attitudes, behaviors, and identities. However, at a societal level, these processes are prone to increase differences between opinion groups and individuals and to cut communication ties between them, leading to what researchers call attitude clusters, social fragmentation, and polarization.[77] In extreme cases, such as the 1994 genocide in Rwanda (see chapter 1), filter bubbles reinforce in-group–out-group tensions to the extent that people are motivated to murder. In more subtle ways, filter bubbles can also get people used to hate speech.

Big Tech companies such as Google, Facebook, and Twitter create rules to moderate content and speech out of a sense of corporate responsibility, but also because their economic viability depends on meeting the community norms of their users.[78] For example, search engines and social media companies have sought to regulate some content on their platforms, such as profanity, violence, and nudity. However, sometimes the best that an algorithm can do is flag an item as a potential violation. When that happens, the company sends the content in question to an employee whose job it is to look at it and decide whether it should be regulated. As users, we do not hear or see these people, but they are filling in where the algorithm has met its limits, to decide whether content is appropriate or not.

A number of scholars have researched the unrecognized

biases of the engineers who create these content-moderation systems. Algorithms are proxies for the people who create them. These peoples' personal beliefs, values, and experiences almost unavoidably find their way into the products they create. This will influence what content is promoted and what content is marginalized or suppressed.

According to the Artificial Intelligence Index Report, the AI workforce remains predominantly male and lacks diversity in race and ethnicity, gender identity, and sexual orientation.[79] Because the AI workforce lacks diversity, the algorithms produced by it often reproduce or reinforce existing inequalities and may disproportionately impact historically marginalized groups.

Research has shown how major media platforms filter online speech in ways that marginalize and stigmatize LGBTQIA+ communities by promoting anti-LGBTQIA+ content in Google News search results. Automated content-moderation processes also systematically demonetize and penalize queer content on YouTube by flagging and removing videos containing LGBTQIA+-related vocabulary.[80] (Recall the earlier discussion of advertising blocklists.) Additionally, LGBTQIA+ folx, trans and nonbinary people, and BIPOC and disabled people tend to experience censorship on Instagram at greater rates than their more privileged counterparts, further highlighting how the identities of people belonging to marginalized groups are policed on social media and other online platforms.[81]

Google searches for images of Black Americans reinforce white supremacist ideology by producing pictures of monkeys, a longstanding anti-Black racist trope in the United States.[82] Problematic search results about marginalized groups reinforce racism, sexism, and homophobia and have real-world implications. Efforts to use Big Tech algorithms to produce equity in educational outcomes have actually worsened educational opportunities for students from a lower socioeconomic status.[83] Similarly, rather than reducing criminal behavior as they promised to do, forty years of data collection using algorithmic systems have actually led to cuts in social services for those who depend on them most.

Safiya Umoja Noble's critical analysis of algorithmic oppression introduces the idea of **digital redlining**, an adaptation of a term originally used to describe how financial institutions classified certain neighborhoods as "hazardous" or not worthy of investment due to the racial makeup of the community's residents. The sociologist John McKnight coined the term **redlining** in the 1960s to describe how this form of systemic discrimination denied home mortgages, loans, insurance, and health care to people, based on where they lived rather than on their individual qualifications. The most significant impacts of redlining have been on economically marginalized communities of color.

Building on the concept of redlining, Noble writes that

various forms of digital redlining are "on the rise."[84] Digital redlining involves both access to online services and the distribution and promotion of media content on the basis of presumed racial identities. As such, digital redlining promotes division along racial lines, just as redlining in bank loans, insurance, and health care previously did. Digital algorithms almost certainly helped amplify the scope of Nicki Minaj's tweets about the COVID-19 vaccine, as discussed in chapter 4. The media coverage of Minaj's tweets subtly served to reinforce racist stereotypes that exemplify points Noble makes about how "digital decisions reinforce oppressive social relationships and enact new modes of racial profiling."[85]

Critical studies of algorithmic bias—including Safiya Umoja Noble's *Algorithms of Oppression* and Virginia Eubanks's *Automating Inequality*—encourage us to be wary of how easy it is to build enduring human prejudices into "neutral" algorithms that, in turn, reproduce deeply rooted inequalities.[86]

Looking to the Future of "Metaverse Literacy"

Let's take a look into the future of one rapidly expanding social technology, the Metaverse, a term coined by the speculative fiction writer Neal Stephenson in his 1992 novel *Snow Crash*. The way most of us engage online through websites and cellphones can be considered a two-dimensional or 2D experience. The **Metaverse** uses augmented reality (AR), mixed reality (MR), and virtual reality (VR) to create an immersive 3D experience. The online game Second Life pioneered some of these virtual social technologies. Today, well-known Metaverse projects include Decentraland, Fortnite, Meta (formerly Facebook), Minecraft, and Roblox, to name just a few. All are owned by Big Tech companies, except Decentraland, which is managed by a nonprofit foundation.[87] The diminishing distinction between online and offline experiences provides a rich opportunity to develop what we could call "Metaverse literacy" awareness.

As introduced in chapter 1, Stuart Hall's encoding-decoding model can be applied to any medium, including the Metaverse. The Metaverse is a growing global digital medium with the potential to perpetuate hegemonic social issues currently plaguing the internet, such as cyberbullying, racism, the commercial sexual exploitation of children, internet addiction, and constant surveillance. As new digital societies emerge, the relationship between government and digital citizens will require radical rethinking. This growing global digital medium may force us to rethink concepts such as the role of identity, laws and governance, ownership of digital property, cybersecurity, and perceptions of space and time.

The latest wave of new technologies is accelerating our transition into a fully immersive Metaverse. We are witnessing these transitions as many important facets of life have "gone digital" and more will do so in the future.

For some of us, our identity is already tied to the digital footprint we leave behind. "If you didn't post it, it didn't happen." Some of us would not dare post a selfie or video without a filter. Some may consider online followers we've never met friends. Now, when young people are told to go play, many will grab a controller or another device before grabbing a ball. The COVID-19 pandemic forced many of us to abandon our office and school to work remotely on our computers or tablets. These are shifts toward the fully immersive Metaverse, where more time is spent connected to and engaging with a device or the internet than is spent connecting to people and experiences in physical reality. As proponents of the Metaverse see it, full immersion will engage all five of our senses, giving participants the perception of real-life experience. It is essential we hold on to the concepts of critical media literacy as we explore the new digital world to come.

Adapting Hall's theory, the Metaverse will be embedded with messages as part of its production. Reina Robinson, the managing director of Center for Urban Excellence (and one of this book's authors), suggests we begin to forecast and define necessary Metaverse literacy skills that should be practiced as we continue our transition into these rapidly advancing technologies. Companies engaged in traditional advertising and marketing methods (discussed further in the next chapter) have gotten a head start. Consider four examples of how corporate power is already shaping the developing Metaverse:

Virtual Events and Experiential Marketing:
Metapalooza, for example, was one of the first Metaverse art and culture festivals to take place across various digital spaces. Also, Fortnite has collaborated with Marvel to make the supervillain Thanos a playable online character, and with music artists whose concert events saw more than 12.3 million concurrent virtual concert goers.[88]

In-Game Products and Purchases: Depictions of everyday items for sale, like clothing and accessories, cosmetology services, and real estate. A recent land transaction on Decentraland sold for $2.4 million.[89] Fortnite emotes are game motions that range from trending dance moves to universal body gestures and actions purchased with V-bucks (originally purchased with fiat currency).

Integrated Advertisements: Methods by which ads are subtly integrated into digital spaces, similar to how ads are integrated into physical reality on billboards and buildings.

Required Log-in Creative Experiences: For example, *Time* magazine and Fortnite collaborated on a Martin Luther King Jr. virtual museum, where they re-created the 1963

Thinking about the Future of Metaverse Literacy

We are headed toward the Metaverse. Think about your process for choosing the profile picture or avatar and username you present on Snapchat, or the effort given to Amazon product reviews. Think about how much time you spend on YouTube, Instagram, or Tik-Tok in a single day. We are increasingly spending more time in digital spaces. Think about what you have learned so far, coupled with your own experiences in the virtual world . . .

◘ How do you think media literacy may need to adapt to the growing use of augmented reality, mixed reality, and virtual reality?

◘ Do you think the physical and virtual are equally significant? If not, do you think we may reach a moment where they become equally significant? How will we recognize that moment?

◘ What roles do privacy, surveillance, and ethics play in the Metaverse?

◘ How do you define identity in the Metaverse?

March on Washington. *Time* introduced the theme as gamers' Fortnite characters loaded. Participants could then bypass the remaining experience once the lobby loaded.

Technology can transform the future of how we perceive, engage in, and make sense of life. While the Metaverse may provide limitless opportunity, we should continue to analyze and understand the powers that shape this growing phenomenon, and to remain critical in the ways we participate. Beyond the Metaverse, other companies and groups will attempt to both colonize and free our imaginations in new ways, and we'll have choices to make.

Putting the Pieces Together: Understanding How Technology "Knows" Us

One place where all this digital and algorithmic literacy might impact you directly is in your school day. Because you most likely go to school daily, Big Tech companies are especially interested in you as a site for data collection. In general, the Big Tech companies are not allowed to collect data about you if you are under the age of eighteen.[90] You and your parents or guardians need to give those companies specific, written permission to gather your data (but when has *that* happened?). However, Big Tech companies bypass this restriction by learning more about you via technologies provided to your classrooms.

Big corporations provide a lot of free or deeply discounted technology—for example, computers, Wi-Fi access, and software programs—to schools and classrooms. Although this can be helpful for students, teachers, and schools, this technology comes with bigger, hidden costs: these tech companies are competing with each other to get more information about you.

For example, Apple and Google compete to get specific technology into schools. Apple provides iPads for use in classrooms and Google provides Chromebooks, both at deeply discounted prices. This is presented as corporate charity: these giant companies swoop in to save struggling schools or schools at risk of falling behind. Both Google and Apple focus on how their respective technologies can enhance learning, cultivate creativity, and help teachers provide much-needed technology skills. But at what cost? What is not widely publicized is that to access these tools, schools and teachers must agree to the terms of service, which means providing unfettered access to user data, including the data of student users.

In addition, Google announced in 2018 that it would spend $300 million to support student journalism projects for middle and high school students to practice news literacy.[91] Although this is great—as advocates of critical media literacy we would never argue *against* increased media literacy!—critically media-literate citizens are also concerned about what it means for the company that controls one of the largest search engines to determine what counts as news literacy: Will Google be self-critical regarding its own practices? Will it look at its own complicity in enabling the circulation of misinformation? Will it discuss its role in online surveillance?

Seeing Multiple Literacies in Advertising

One element that gets woven into all this "free" software and hardware is advertising. Advertisements show up in both obvious and subtle ways: they can be as overt as a break in content or as imperceptible as brand awareness—for example, seeing (and recognizing) a logo when a character in your favorite show wears a certain shoe brand. Advancements in digital technology have allowed advertising to become much subtler; we might not even need breaks in content in order to see advertisements anymore, because they are so easily woven into the content. While these big companies focus on gathering information about you, they also make sure that you know the parts about them that they want you to know.

CHAPTER 6

Advertising and Consumerism

Ads Are Everywhere

You're scrolling through your Instagram feed when there it is—suddenly, a company is trying to sell you their latest body wash. Sure, you can scroll right by, but the video starts and grabs your attention. Or you click on a YouTube video, but have to watch five seconds of an advertisement about a new gaming system first. It does not matter where you go, what feed you're on, or whether you are watching regular old television. Ads are everywhere. Media citizens not only analyze advertising content but ask these questions: Why are ads everywhere? Who produces them? How are they produced? What is their purpose?

To advertisers, and even to some extent to the people who create TV shows, television is just a vehicle for putting ads in front of the viewer.[92] Or, more to the point, it's a vehicle for putting viewers in front of ads. You, the viewer, are what TV producers are selling to their advertisers, who pay more depending on how many "eyeballs" the producers can deliver. And this is true for social media as well, because really, you are the product. Producers and creators make content or an experience that keeps you on the screen, and companies pay social media and television companies to lob ads at you through your screen and speakers. Social media apps are free. But they are not. They seem to be "free" because we do not pay anything to use them. But these apps are financed by advertising, and we "pay" to use them by giving their products and services our time and our attention.

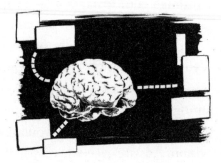

However, it's more complex than that. It's not just that your eyeballs are being sold to the highest bidder. It's not just that your attention is being captured. It's that your eyes, your attention, are the path to your mind. And what is being sold to us? What is taking hold in our minds? Advertising conditions us into *desires* and *behaviors*: the need to have the newest, latest whatever-it-is; the need to look as good as the celebrities who sell us beauty products;

the need to be as popular, as stylish, as cool as the people next to us. But "next to us" does not mean what it did twenty, ten, or even five years ago.

Advertisements condition our understanding of ourselves in the context of "everyone else." Our venues for this comparison—finding ourselves not as cool, not as stylish, not as popular—are no longer just our classrooms and our neighborhoods. Today, our mobile devices provide virtual "spaces" for seeing ourselves negatively in relation to others. We no longer have to visit these spaces: they are sitting in our pockets, waiting for us to go "visit" them. This has a deep impact not only on individual thought but on how society operates. Our sense of self is altered, or built differently than it would be without the omnipresence of advertising.

Advertising—media messages intended to inform audiences about a product, service, or cause, with the ultimate aim of convincing audience members that they *need* to buy those products and services, or to invest in those causes—is everywhere. You cannot just avoid it. So what can you do? Well, the first thing is to start paying attention to *how* advertisers enter your mind. The strategies and principles of advertising are the gears that make the clock go, and once you "see" the gears, you will understand better how they are being manipulated to alter, and probably ramp up, your purchasing habits, and even how you see yourself as a person. Then you will begin to have the foundation for critically evaluating advertisements.

Advertising is a multibillion-dollar industry: in late December 2020, marketing analysts projected that global ad spending for 2021 would be around $600 billion, with US ad spending hovering near $225 billion.[93] That's more money than most of us can imagine. For comparison, in 2019, global movie sales amounted to $42.5 billion and video game revenue was around $138.7 billion, while in the previous year worldwide sales of athletic shoes reached $58 billion.[94]

All that money would not be swirling around if ads did not work. They do. And over the decades, advertisers have developed better and better methods for seizing you by the eyeballs and holding your attention. Of course, what happens in your mind once they have your attention is not the same for everyone: According to Stuart Hall's encoding-decoding model (see chapter 1), no matter the sender's intended message, as receivers of the message we do not all interpret it the same way. We are free to accept or reject an advertisement's intended message. So we want to empower you to negotiate your relationship with advertisements and consumerism.

Seeing Behind the Ads

Media citizens understand that the craft of influencing media users is not magic. Advertisers use a limited set of strategies and techniques to influence users. A media citizen may be less susceptible to advertising because they can

identify these strategies, understand how they work, and
act to counter their influence.

Underlying the specific advertising strategies are two
concepts that we might call guiding principles. The first is
what the media professor Bernard McGrane calls the **production of discontent**. That is, advertisements commonly
suggest or operate on the premise that there is something
wrong with you, some flaw that can be solved only by
your buying and using the product they are advertising.[95]
The second principle is **emotional transfer**; this is when
advertisers foster feelings in audiences, through the advertisement's "plot" or imagery, and then transfer that emotion
to the product or brand. They get you to feel *something*,
generally, then they attach that feeling to the product.

Think about a product that you really like or really dislike: Is it possible that those feelings come from the story of the product presented in the ad? Or take a look at almost any car ad: the folks in the ad are having fun in the car; maybe they are driving around laughing, listening to tunes. It does not matter what the car's features are; it matters that they are carefree and having *fun*. This is sneaky, but it's only one of the tricks that advertisers use.

There are more than thirty common persuasive advertising strategies that critical-media-literacy educators identify and explore with students, but you can also learn to recognize these on your own. Once you are able to do that, you can see through advertisers' tricks! Here are a few of the most common, some of which you may recognize as overlapping with many of the common logical fallacies and biases introduced in chapter 2:[96]

Bandwagon: "Everybody's doing it!" Showing us that doing or having a certain thing is popular, which makes us want to do or have that thing so we can be members of the cool crowd.

Beautiful people: Attractive people using the product or enjoying the product together, using beauty and people we admire to sell us products or lifestyles (because depicting an attractive lifestyle is central to so much advertising).

Testimonial: Famous or respected people—a celebrity you like or an expert you admire and believe—talking about or showing how great the product is.

Simple solutions: Playing on the production of discontent, if you get this product, you'll be smarter or more attractive, you'll lose weight, you'll grow muscles, you'll attract people you find attractive . . . Just buy this product, and your problems are solved!

Big lie: Can be explicit lies (cigarettes were once marketed as being *healthy*) or more implied or suggested, such as the idea that the product will make you look as good as a photo-edited model. (In fact, most modeling images are big lies: the documentary *Killing Us Softly* illustrates how an image of a single model may actually be Photoshopped images of multiple women's body parts, morphed into one body.)[97] The big lie is one of the tools that direct us to examine propaganda (as we do in chapter 7).

Either-or: Presenting situations in black and white, or what is known as **binary thinking**, a version of the logical fallacy known as the **false dilemma**. It presents situations with only two outcomes (positive and negative) when in reality there are multiple possibilities.

Humor: What is better at catching our attention than remembering funny moments in our lives? Advertising that uses humor often plays on this desire.

Repetition is also a common technique within ads, but it deserves its own mention as a tool of advertising more generally. Advertisements are repeated over time: if you watch a certain show every week, you will notice that specific ads get repeated over and over again. Obviously, if you see the same thing over and over again, it sticks in your head, and that's what advertisers want.

Of course, sometimes we also want to buy a particular product or service because we genuinely like what is being sold. We have tried it, or friends have told us about it and we have checked it out, and we have decided we want it. There is nothing wrong with that. But critical media literacy provides us with tools to understand and act upon the impact of media consumption; these advertising tools help us to take a deeper look at our own consumerism.

Cracking Consumer Culture

Consumer culture is one in which money and behaviors revolve around the consumption of products and services. Our entire economy is built around production and consumption, so for it to succeed, people need to buy, buy, and buy more. We do not buy simply for practical reasons—to get stuff we need—but also to feel satisfied, to look a certain way, or to compete with peers, to have things we *desire*. Living in a consumer culture makes us feel that we must buy things, because the more stuff we have, the better we are. Of course, many of us genuinely enjoy what we buy. The problem arises when we're buying things not because we like them or need them but in order to show off or meet a certain societal expectation. In the middle of the twentieth century, there was a well-known concept that illustrated consumer culture: keeping up with the Joneses. This meant that people would keep their house a certain way, or they would buy a certain car, or they would wear a certain suit, all in order to be on par with their neighbors, to hold a status similar to the people around them.

Consumer culture today consists of similar behaviors. Consider the role of influencers in our social media and, specifically, the impact such celebrities have on our purchasing habits.

If we pay attention to influencers, then we might buy or want to buy the things they suggest we buy, or the products we believe will make us look like, or otherwise seem like, the people we admire. Influencers are, of course, advertisers, or the tools of advertisers. They create **sponsored content**, or sponcon. They are paid to sell or speak highly of certain products, because manufacturers know that influencers have power over you and me, the buyers. The advertising is embedded in the posts of influencers whose accounts we have chosen to follow; we are giving away our attention, and sometimes we do not even get that we are being targeted by advertisers (see chapter 3 for more on influencers). The Western world is based on consumer culture, but a successful consumer culture does not just happen. It requires manipulation of the marketplace, of the buyers. For our purposes, the two primary tools for this manipulation are advertising and branding.

If we look at advertising campaigns, series of ads for the same product or family of products, we begin to see that there is more going on than just selling specific items. Companies engage in **branding**, forming identities for themselves through the way they present their products to the buying public. Once these identities are formed, or as they are formed, advertising also works to create **brand loyalty**, leading customers to prefer a particular brand (company) or product over others produced by competing companies, often seemingly regardless of quality. Why, for instance, do some people prefer Macs to PCs, or the other way around? For most users, laptops of both kinds provide the same functions. Unless they have specialized skills or interests, most users choose their product based on brand loyalty. As of mid-2021 Apple owns about 16 percent of the computer market, and their users are vocal about it.[98] They are *loyal*. A Mac owner is unlikely to go and buy a Samsung phone; they're probably going to buy an iPhone. This loyalty can even be fostered at a young age, through computers provided to students at school. In any case, this loyalty, this buying preference, is the result of deeply clever branding developed over the last forty years. A brand is an identity, and consumers often tie their own personal identities to corporate brands. They *identify* with the brand. And this creates *profit* because identification amounts to brand loyalty. Loyal Apple customers will buy Apple products almost exclusively, year after year.

Our economic system is predicated on profit, consumption, and competition: we make stuff and buy stuff. Walk into Walmart. Go to any aisle. What do you see? Multiple versions of the same product from different companies. In any grocery store or section, you might see, say, twenty-seven kinds of chocolate chip cookies. We do not *need* all of those. Maybe we "need" four or five: some handmade, some factory-manufactured, some organic, some not. But our economies, it seems, need this level of *stuff* to exist. We need factories to make this stuff; we need products moving through markets; people need to earn money to live. This is not the only way to organize an economy, but it is the organization we have. In short, the economy *is* production and consumption. If we are not *making and buying*, then our economy is not "healthy."

Why does all this matter? Who cares? If the economy is good, then people have jobs, right? If we have jobs, we can pay our rent, buy food for our families, pay for heat or air conditioning, afford a car, and yes, even do the fun stuff we like to do. But how have we landed in a place where we think that fun is necessarily tied to *buying*? How have we come to a place where who we are is grounded in buying and having *stuff*?

Stealing Our Attention, Stealing Our Minds

The answer lies in our economic model, which depends on three premises that are so fundamental we typically take them for granted, as being "natural" or inevitable: (1) private ownership of property, (2) a social relationship between workers and employers in which workers sell their labor power to employers in return for a wage, and (3) the goal of maximizing profits. Advertising has played an essential role in building our profit-maximizing economy. If we understand advertising, we can begin a critique of consumer culture. In turn, that critique can help us start to consider (and imagine) different economic models that might encourage other ways of knowing ourselves beyond the narrow, market-based roles of employers and employees, producers and consumers.

In a consumer culture, it can be difficult for an advertiser to promote their product, service, or brand when every other advertiser is also competing for your attention. This results in the creation of an **attention economy**, which develops when businesses, especially media and technology companies, compete for the attention of (potential) consumers. Social media plays a key role here: users' attention is sold to advertising companies, which means your attention is the product that companies such as Google and Facebook are selling for billions to other businesses that have products to push.

Users are bombarded with ads, often without a way to stop them. Consider how we consume music in the twenty-first century. Spotify and other music-streaming apps make money in two ways: advertisers pay them to run ads, and some listeners pay for a membership to avoid hearing ads. Either way, the service gets paid. Like social media channels, streaming services are free in name only. Companies operate on this principle: we want your attention, and you want our product; pay us directly or pay us by proxy (through our advertisers). Social media and consumption of goods—purchasing—are where we put our *attention*.

The American philosopher and psychologist William James wrote that "everyone knows what attention is. It is the taking possession by the mind, in clear and vivid form, of one out of what seem several simultaneously possible objects or trains of thought."[99] In other words, attention is focus. But is our focus always an active choice? The legal scholar and Biden administration official for technology competition Tim Wu says that "the study of attention is the study of conscious experience and our very sense of existence."[100] When you consider that social media is where we so often build our sense of self and present that self to the world, you can perhaps appreciate concerns about how consumerism drives our behaviors and shapes our identities. Our *sense of existence* becomes intertwined with what we consume, with what we allow to have our attention: social media feeds, internet ads, those sneakers we simply must have, arguments online with people we will never meet. Remember "keeping up with the Joneses"? We do that these days through our online presence, not just through what we buy but also where we find it and how we share it. Not only do companies compete for our attention and then buy and sell our personal histories as consumers to other companies, but we compete for *each other's attention*. Our very selves become the currency of this new economy.[101] On social media platforms such as Facebook and Instagram, for instance, our sense of self-worth may be significantly influenced by the number of followers we have, how many "likes" or views our posts receive, and whether other people take the time to comment on or share what we've posted.

Wu explains that either we can choose where to focus our attention or it "can be seized." He refers to this seizing of our attention alternately as attentional intrusion (although seizure comes in other forms, like being drawn to a screen held by another person), attention theft, and attentional larceny.[102] He uses criminal language deliberately, because he is a legal scholar concerned with regulation and protection. And he seems to want to shock us into doing something about it. So while we *can* make choices based on our own preferences, we too often do not. He refers to advertising as non-consensual and intrusive, which takes us right back to the examples that kick off this chapter: ads in your feeds that you do not ask for and do not want. But we can just scroll on by, right? Well, no. On YouTube, for instance, even if we want to avoid ads, we have to watch five seconds' worth before being allowed to click "skip ad." And on TikTok, we cannot scroll past the ad for at least a few seconds. But, you might say, on some social media channels, you can in fact just scroll by, so where's the harm? As Wu says, "Advertisements with motion and sound are difficult if not impossible to ignore due to the involuntary attentional responses of the brain."[103] So even if we think we are scrolling by, and even if the ad is static, our attention is at least partly drawn, and our brain is flooded with information that we did not choose to absorb. Our attention is *stolen*. Certainly, we could all come up with accidental value that comes from our attention being stolen, but that seems like a stretch. At best, all this advertising clutters our brains. At worst, it creates or reinforces images that are damaging to our self-image and our perceptions of the world (recall chapter 4 on representations). What positive value does modern advertising have to the *consumer*? Not much. The value belongs to the advertisers and manufacturers: it brings in dollars. But stealing our attention damages us.

There is harm in the removal of our agency, our power to choose how to spend our time, but there is also damage to cognitive function: when people consume media, there is what is called a **substitution effect**, a "crowding-out of alternative activities."[104] We consume media instead of doing things that might be more valuable, or valuable in other ways. We also know now that multitasking is a myth, and that when we switch from one task to another (or worse, one project to another), it takes about twenty-three minutes (on average) to refocus and get back to where we were. This can also create "higher levels of stress, frustration, mental effort, feeling of time pressure and mental workload."[105] And it is well-known that these negative feelings affect not only our well-being but also our productivity and focus.

According to Wu, we need to embrace good attention, which is "deep, long-lasting and voluntary," instead of bad attention, which is "quick, superficial and often involuntarily provoked."[106] We need good attention to become our best selves, which means we need less bad attention. So how do we address this without adopting a **protectionist** stance (as described in chapter 2), without abandoning our media consumption?

What Can *I* Do? What Can *We* Do?

We can reclaim our minds and our time, our energy and our relationships. As critically media-literate citizens, we can reframe the problem and find our own modes of resistance to advertisers and advertising-driven content.

(1) On our own, we can create or find activities that require a certain depth of attention and seriousness, as Wu suggests. This could help us find freedom from advertising, and we could discover or rediscover some things we enjoy doing without the *buy, buy, buy* pressure and mentality.

Read a book (a comic, a graphic novel, a magazine . . .)! Go on hikes or bike rides! Play a board game (without digital enhancements)! Learn with expert friends or loved ones how to replace the family car's carburetor! Start a garden

in containers or in the backyard! Make your own music by learning to play an instrument![107]

(2) We can look to organizations like Adbusters for ideas.[108] They have a regular newsletter, and they list actions such as protests in the newsletter and on their website. We can join in these actions, or we can be inspired to create actions within our own communities, with groups of friends in physical spaces or affinity groups that gather in digital space. Adbusters can show us paths to finding folks who share our concerns and who, like us, want to act. This can lead us to the "we" in "What can *we* do?"

(3) For a more direct route into media activism, we can consider engaging in **culture jamming**, or **subvertising**. Jammers manipulate existing advertising or marketing images and text in order to critique not only mass media

Culture Jamming Is Political and Social Expression that Disrupts

Culture jamming allows for alternative communication strategies that subvert mainstream ideologies and institutions. Who are culture jammers you recognize? Find an example of culture jamming, a subvertisement, or a meme, and dissect it:

◘   What mainstream narrative is it subverting?

◘   How does this expression challenge social norms and break the rules of tradition?

◘   What values, ideologies, or institutions are being criticized?

◘   How does the work uncover forms of oppression that might otherwise remain unrecognized?

◘   How does this subversive expression undermine the brand or institution?

messaging but the corporate agenda and underlying structures *behind* those messages. Today, a familiar form of culture jamming is meme creation. This **"brandalism"**—vandalizing of brands, or the images that are key to a corporation's success—is satire, critical-media-literacy action with a wry chuckle.

Vandalism as a critique of power is nothing new: Graffiti artists have done this for a long time. But brandalism, as a movement and a form of public action, takes that a step farther, using reworked images to create new, anti-capitalist messaging.

Be aware, though, that culture jammers in the streets are doing something illegal; instead, you should jam as an arts-and-crafts project, on your social media feeds, or in other digital spaces.

Advertising's Influence on Journalism

Of course, advertising's influence is not limited to its effect on audiences or its role in the persistence of consumer culture. It also plays a fundamental role in journalism. Advertising has a long and complex relationship with news and journalism. The most profound effects of advertising on news coverage are largely "invisible" effects—the news stories that do not get covered, the important perspectives on current events that are omitted or marginalized. We've already considered how advertising interests can mute coverage of humanitarian crises (recall the discussion of advertising blocklists from chapter 5). To extend this critical inquiry, consider how the business interests of the corporations that manufacture weapons of war might affect coverage of the 2022 Russian invasion of Ukraine.

The Pulitzer Prize-winning journalist Chris Hedges argues that the economic interests of weapons manufacturers have a profound impact on US news coverage of the Ukraine crisis. In a March 2022 interview, Hedges described war as "demonic," and he went on to explain that war is not "politics by other means" (as is often claimed); instead, war is about "the destruction of all systems that nurture and protect life: environmental, social, cultural, political, familial, religious."[109] As the Real News Network reported in an interview with Hedges, "While debates about the war in Ukraine center on the motivations of Putin and NATO powers, the merchants of death profiting from war are—literally—making a killing."

In this interview Hedges explained that fueling conflict in Ukraine and expanding NATO are "good for business," especially for weapons manufacturers, such as General Dynamics, Lockheed Martin, Northrop Grumman, and

Raytheon, which each benefited from "fifty-two-week highs" in profits after Russia invaded Ukraine.[110] War, Hedges went on to explain, is "sanitized and censored by the news media," a theme he explored in greater detail in his 2002 nonfiction book, *War Is a Force That Gives Us Meaning*.[111] Media coverage of war, including the fighting in Ukraine, removes all the sensory elements of killing and "distorts the reality of war," Hedges told the Real News Network. "If you broadcast real images of war it would be impossible to wage war."

CHAPTER 7

News and Journalism

The Role of the Press

In the summer of 2020, somewhere between 15 and 26 million people in the United States participated in Black Lives Matter (BLM) protests following the murder of George Floyd.[112] Floyd was murdered by a police officer in his community in Minneapolis, Minnesota. Some estimated that the protests were among the largest in US history.[113] Presumably, most of the protesters and activists never met

Floyd or visited his community. So how did they come to know about his murder? How did they come to learn about his community? How did millions of Americans come to learn about the prevalence of racism in their country? Part of the answer is the media. Whether it be Darnella Frazier, the teenager who filmed the murder on her phone, the social media posts from the community, or the news stories about the events, media informed millions of peoples' reactions to Floyd's murder.

The potential for the media to inform and influence us both individually and as a society is exactly why the news media are constitutionally protected. In the United States, the **press**, which refers to journalists and news outlets, are protected from government censorship and persecution by the First Amendment to the United States Constitution. In a democracy, the press is worthy of such protections because without the free flow of information, people cannot make informed decisions about politics and public policy. Chances are a news report has shaped your decision about what political leaders you oppose or support, and whether to sign petitions, volunteer for a particular campaign, or participate in political protests. Media citizens investigate news content and the processes of news production to understand how they inform and influence individuals, communities, and society.

The constitutional protections for the press are designed to help you be a more well-informed and active citizen. The press is entrusted to inform and serve members of society by fulfilling five democratic functions:

Marketplace of Ideas: The press offers a diverse set of facts, perspectives, and ideas for voters to consider when making their democratic decisions. But contemporary news outlets have evolved to cater their content to individual political parties in the United States, often leading to a decrease in diverse representations.

Agenda Setter: The press directs the public's focus on key issues and events. In 1965, Ralph Nader published a best-selling book, *Unsafe at Any Speed*, that drew public attention to the insufficient safety features of automobiles at the time. Press coverage spurred congressional action to require that the automobile industry improve basic safety features, including the car seat belts that we now take for granted.

Watchdog: The press exposes corruption and holds the powerful accountable. For example, the infamous Watergate scandal, which resulted in the resignation of former President Nixon, was exposed by the work of investigative journalists Bob Woodward and Carl Bernstein at the *Washington Post*.

Information Disseminator: The press has long acted as a tool of communication between the public and elected officials. But today, politicians and elected officials often have their own social media accounts, which serve as alternate means of communication with the public. How might this impact the role of the press? What about the quality of information we have access to?

Public Mobilization: The press convinces the public about the policies and issues that are so important they require the public's involvement. For instance, multiple news organizations have led efforts to protect net neutrality, encouraging the public to oppose government legislation against it.

The individual journalists and news outlets that make up the press as an institution are entrusted to carry out these functions. Whether or not they actually do so, or how successfully they serve the public interest, is another matter. These issues were introduced in chapter 3. We will explore them here in more detail, specifically focusing on journalism and the news.

Journalists and Journalism

For their part, journalists aspire to **objectivity**, seeking to provide the public with relevant facts and newsworthy reports. Journalists collect information from their sources, whom they also protect. Those sources are then fact-checked and vetted by editors before being presented to the public. Journalists use five criteria to determine whether something is newsworthy:

- ☑ Is it new or timely?

- ☑ Is it unusual?

- ☑ Is it interesting to the target audience?

- ☑ Is it broadly significant?

- ☑ Does it have a human-interest angle?

However, just because something is newsworthy does not automatically mean it should be published.

The press has influence in this country, and with great influence comes great responsibility. Journalists are often faced with ethical questions and dilemmas. If a journalist has a story about a crime that is being plotted, should they report on it or give the information to law enforcement? Or if they know that the government is going to perform a military operation overseas, illegal or otherwise, should they report on it? To help guide these types of decisions, journalists, like many professions, have a code of ethics that helps them decide whether it is right to publish a particular piece of content. According to the Society of Professional Journalists, the practice of journalism is rooted in four main principles, which date back to 1926 but have been revised over the years. These advise that ethical journalists ought to:

- **Seek truth and report it:** Ethical journalism should be accurate and fair. Journalists should be honest and courageous in gathering, reporting, and interpreting information;

- **Minimize harm:** Ethical journalism treats sources, subjects, colleagues, and members of the public as human beings deserving of respect;

- **Act independently:** The highest and primary obligation of ethical journalism is to serve the public;

- **Be accountable and transparent:** Ethical journalism means taking responsibility for one's work, responding quickly to questions about accuracy, clarity, and fairness, and exposing unethical conduct in journalism.

Journalists are expected to make ethical determinations about their work. However, although individual journalists make choices, they do so in the context of organizations that encourage some types of behavior and discourage others. There are organizational incentives to cover certain kinds of stories in certain ways; and there are organizational constraints that discourage coverage of other issues, topics, and figures. These incentives and constraints act as *institutional* checks on journalists' *individual* actions and beliefs. It is important to distinguish between individual distortions of information based on personal bias versus institutional or organizational biases, or **slant**.

Filtered News and the Propaganda Model

While we want to convey the important role and contributions of the press, it is also crucial to understand that not all news is unvarnished truth. Just like the clock we discussed in the introduction, there is a lot that goes on behind the scenes to shape the news. Journalists who work for news organizations such as the *New York Times* submit their reporting to editors who decide about the validity of the content and whether or not it should be published. Editors can be a journalist's best friend, ensuring that their reporting is accurate, is well supported, and lives up to professional ethics. Editors can also be a source of frustration as they critique weaknesses in journalists' reporting and assert the interests of the company they work for, which may not always be the same as the public interest.

The consolidation of media ownership in recent decades has raised concerns about the manipulation of news content in the editorial process. More specifically, as noted in chapter 3, news media ownership has consolidated significantly: as of 2020, six corporations control roughly 90 percent of the news media in the United States, whereas forty years ago approximately 50 companies controlled a similar market share.[114] This process is known as **conglomeration**.

In their 1988 book, *Manufacturing Consent*, Edward Herman and Noam Chomsky studied how corporate media conglomeration shapes news content.[115] With fewer and fewer outlets deciding what counts as "news," Herman and Chomsky proposed their famous Propaganda Model. They argued news produced by corporate-owned media reflect elite interests, because news content undergoes a "filtering" process that involves ownership, advertising, sourcing (newsmakers and news shapers), flak (criticism), and ideological bias. Herman and Chomsky argued that these five filters restrict the definitions of what and who count as newsworthy in ways that benefit people in power. For these reasons, it does not make sense to talk about corporate news media as "mainstream" news.

In the first two filters, they argue that corporations avoid publishing content that is critical of the interests of ownership or advertisers, because they want the public to have a positive view of both. Think back to our discussion of media and corporate ownership. The media and publishing company News Corp owns the *New York Post*, a newspaper and tabloid organization. News Corp, which also owns Fox News, is headed by Rupert Murdoch, so it's likely that the *New York Post* would not publish content critical of Rupert Murdoch or Fox News. Critical reporting could turn the audience against either or both, which would result in lost revenues. Similarly,

Sources as a News Filter

According to Herman and Chomsky's Propaganda Model, the decisions journalists make about whom to treat as newsworthy sources are one way that news serves elite interests. Because journalists typically treat powerful public figures as their most favored news sources, Herman and Chomsky suggest that news focuses narrowly on what those in power do and say.

You can test Herman and Chomsky's proposal by looking at news stories with a focus on who is quoted in them. Pick a news story of interest to you and find every quotation in the story. For each quotation, note how the quoted person is identified. You will probably find that almost every quoted source is identified by name and job title (e.g., the senator from New York, the White House press secretary, or a spokesperson for Google). Keep track of the variety of job titles or other ways that sources are described.

- ◘ How many of the sources quoted in the article you analyzed are government or corporate officials?
- ◘ How many represent other types of organizations?

■ How many (if any) are identified in terms of family relations or other personal characteristics?

You can also compare and contrast news articles on the same topic from different news organizations, using the same approach. Doing so, you can test Herman and Chomsky's model, and you can also assess how inclusive or exclusive different news organizations are in their coverage of a news topic that interests you.

a company is not going to pay advertising fees to be on a news program that criticizes its products or services.

According to the third filter, sourcing, news media rely on people in positions of power as their sources rather than average, everyday people. Journalists are especially likely to seek out sources who hold official positions in government agencies or corporate organizations. As a result, news stories often reflect the interests of powerful officials in government or corporate roles, rather than the majority of people.

The fourth filter argues that news outlets decide about reporting based on whether or not they will get flak—which means criticism—for their reporting. This means sometimes avoiding fact-based stories because such coverage may upset powerful people or organizations.

As a result, the fifth filter explains that corporate news promotes the dominant ideology by highlighting potential threats—whether real, exaggerated, or imagined—and framing them in terms of "us" versus "them" (recall the discussion of in-group–out-group dynamics from chapter 1).

Overall, Herman and Chomsky understand filtered news as a form of **propaganda**, which works through controlled transmission of one-sided messages (which may or may not be factual) via mass and direct media channels. Filtered news is propaganda designed to persuade its audience to accept the views and interests of a ruling elite as their own.

In this view, corporate news functions more to benefit the powerful and to maximize profits than to serve democracy. Essentially, the audience receives limited information because the press as an institution narrows the so-called marketplace of ideas and the information that they disseminate to the perspectives and points that prove profitable.

More than the *personal* bias of *individual* journalists, the filters identified by Herman and Chomsky suggest how news is subject to *systemic organizational* biases. As Steve Macek and Andy Lee Roth of Project Censored have summarized, the "self-interest and partisan bias of editors and journalists" cannot fully explain the power of news. Instead, Macek and Roth suggest, "understanding the establishment media's deepest biases, not to mention the power of news more generally, requires a structural analysis of journalism, including the economic imperatives, institutional constraints, professional values and social relationships that shape the production of every news story."[116] This is exactly what Herman and Chomsky's Propaganda Model addresses.

That said, media citizens such as yourself should not only be concerned about individual or institutional biases but also mindful of their own biases (as discussed in chapter 2). By the 1990s, programming research revealed that news audiences were more likely to tune in when news reports confirmed their own views, a situation referred to as **confirmation bias**, and their political positions were treated as morally superior to the opposition's. In response, instead of addressing a general audience of diverse people, news outlets targeted more specific demographics based on political affiliation. News organizations abandoned unbiased, objective reporting in favor of stories that emphasized partisan bias in order to build distinctive brands and audience bases, which also ensured certain profits and market shares. The resulting content was largely hyper-partisan. The *New York Times*, the *Washington Post*, CNN, and MSNBC became megaphones for the Democratic Party, and they faced off against Fox News, the *Wall Street Journal*, and the *New York Post* as mouthpieces of the Republican Party. Now more people choose news that confirms their views rather than challenges them, making it less likely they will encounter new information about what's happening in the world around them. Confirmation bias, as well as **motivated reasoning** and **inferred justification** (again, back to chapter 2), can pose real challenges when attempting to help others see the impacts of propaganda, because it can be difficult for us to see it ourselves. Today, many people obtain a portion of their news from social media platforms; how might confirmation bias affect the information you see on your feed, if it is coming primarily from those you follow and with whom you align?

You should be mindful that, although the information they peddle is not necessarily false or inaccurate, corporate news media carefully choose and shape content to reflect the political interests of a particular party and its members. **Spin**—a twist put on a story to influence the audience's interpretation—is so common that many events, such as campaign speeches and political debates, include "spin rooms" where public relations firms seek to inform how members of the press report on the performances and speech of elected officials or political candidates. Although the news media is supposed to "unspin" the content for the public, sometimes they report the spin as content.

In addition to spin, critical media literacy alerts us to the role of **slant**—the framing of news reports and editorials in ways that favor one side over others in current or potential disputes—in shaping news content. Scholars who research news slant find that it persists across time, news topics, and different news outlets. This indicates how news media may *systematically* help distribute power to particular groups, causes, or individuals.[117]

When you encounter news content, look for techniques that news producers use to support or oppose a political party, or simply to protect those in power. The political scientist Michael Parenti summed up some of the practices used to inflame hyper-partisanship and further spin or manipulate information. These include suppression by omission (censorship, passive or active), attacking and labeling a target (*ad hominem*, overgeneralization), preemptive assumption (stereotyping, status quo bias), face-value transmission (accepting claims without questioning), slighting of content (selective limitations of information), false balancing (hearing from "both sides" when one has clearly already been proven), follow-up avoidance (not asking further questions), and framing (defining limits of information and perceptions open to debate). Some of these concepts clearly intersect with the fallacies explored in chapter 2 and relate to misinformation, disinformation, and propaganda as well.

The failures of news media and their propensity to sometimes stoke bias and fear have not been lost on Americans. After the 2020 election, about 57 percent of Democrats and 18 percent of Republicans trusted the news media. 2021 marked the first year that less than half of the American public overall, around 40 percent, trusted the news media. This may help explain the recent trends that indicate audiences are abandoning legacy media—pre-digital-era media outlets, such as newspapers and network television news—for digital sources. For example, in the first hundred days following the inauguration of President Biden, legacy media audiences shrank, with outlets such as the *New York Times*, MSNBC, and CNN losing a fifth, fourth, and half of their audience, respectively.[118] Meanwhile, the portion of Americans who rely on social media and YouTube for their news has surpassed the number of us who turn to newspapers. This trend is not limited to younger audiences, but includes older generations, and scholars have noted that many of the same problems regarding news media manipulation are simply replicated in digital spaces.

Some have argued that the ways in which news media provide limited and sometimes distorted information is an act of censorship because it comes at the expense of the press's function as a marketplace of ideas. How can news outlets claim to be information disseminators when they limit the marketplace of ideas to a narrow agenda? **Censorship** refers to the suppression of speech, public communication, or other information on the grounds that it is objectionable, harmful, or sensitive. The First Amendment to the US Constitution protects the press from censorship by the government, but it does not address news censorship by corporate owners. In fact, the news media have sometimes been caught censoring information for the government. For these reasons, the news watchdog Project Censored—which includes a number of the authors of this book—recommends a broader definition of censorship as "anything that interferes with the free flow of information in a society that purports to have a free press system."[119] Each year, Project Censored publishes a list of the most important independent news stories that corporate media have either covered in biased ways or entirely ignored. These "censored" story lists demonstrate corporate news media's extremely narrow definitions of who and what count as "newsworthy," suggesting that Herman and Chomsky's propaganda model is on target.[120]

It's upsetting to think that censorship occurs in what we like to think of as a free society. Fortunately, there are ways to push back against news media manipulation.

Fighting Media Manipulation

Like many citizens around the world, you may be concerned about media manipulation. It was digital news content, referred to as "fake news," that spurred international concern that false news reports were misleading voters after the so-called Brexit vote in the United Kingdom and the election of President Donald Trump in the United States. Trump weaponized the term "fake news" to denounce any reporting he deemed to be inaccurate or inconveniently critical of him or his administration. However, Jennifer Allen and colleagues explain that fake news is "broadly defined as false or misleading information masquerading as legitimate news."[121] As Nolan Higdon (one of this book's authors) notes in *The Anatomy of Fake News: A Critical News Literacy Education*, "Fake news is anything but self-explanatory. It extends far beyond news itself and exists in numerous formats such as rumors, lies, hoaxes, bunk, satire, parody, misleading content, impostor content, fabricated content, and manipulated content."[122] You may have seen examples of this in the form of click-bait, or snappy titles designed to grab your attention, which often leave out crucial details of the story itself. For example, you may see titles with wording such as "You'll Never Believe . . ." or "The Real Reason . . ." followed by the names of influential people or events. The sensation-alized nature of clickbait can affect how audiences make sense of the information that follows. The power of fake news should not be underestimated; it has the potential to mislead and misinform the public in detrimental ways. The most effective fake news circumvents critical thinking by appealing to lower human emotions of hate and fear.

You are not powerless against the influence of the news media, however. As a critically news-literate person you can investigate news content and the process behind its produc-tion and dissemination. One way to begin is to familiarize yourself with who is likely to produce fake news.

The known producers of fake news include the following:

The Legacy Media: These are often called "mainstream" media, but are also sometimes referred to as "corporate" media. Although they reach large audiences and report on many daily affairs accurately, they sometimes report falsehoods that can be minor, such as misattributing a quote, or significant, such as the claim that Iraq possessed weapons of mass destruction, which served as one justification for the catastrophic US invasion of Iraq in 2003.

State-sponsored propaganda machines: A conglomerate of government-funded efforts that seek to influence public opinion. Governments, including the United States, have long produced and distributed fake news to domestic and foreign populations through outlets such as Radio Televisión Martí and Voice of America. Other nations, including Russia, engage in propaganda operations that also seek to shape global interpretations of events.

Political party propaganda apparatuses: Loosely connected groups that work to influence electoral outcomes and policy debates through the promotion of content including fake news. These organizations include public relations firms and members of the news media who often work in tandem. For example, elements of the Republican Party and conservative media such as the One America News network (OAN) and Fox News

Channel coordinated in 2020 to normalize the "Stop the Steal" campaign, which argued that the Democrats had stolen the 2020 presidential election from Donald Trump. Similarly, for four years during Trump's presidency, the Democratic Party perpetuated elements of the Russiagate scandal that proved to be false—such as claims that the Russians shut down a Vermont power plant, infiltrated Bernie Sanders's 2020 campaign, hacked Democratic Party emails, put bounties on US soldiers' heads, and offered Trump's campaign adviser, George Papadopoulos, compromising information on Clinton—to delegitimize Trump's presidency.

Satirical fake news: A form of entertainment that lampoons dominant culture by simulating a major news outlet's format and presentation. Examples include *The Onion, Last Week Tonight with John Oliver*, and *Full Frontal with Samantha Bee*.

Self-interested actors: People who create fake news to serve their own ends. For example, in an effort to promote his own career, Jayson Blair reported fake news in numerous stories he filed while he worked at the *New York Times* and *Boston Globe*. He is hardly the only reporter to do so. Others include Stephen Glass of the *New Republic*, Brian Williams of MSNBC, Bill O'Reilly of Fox News Channel, and the American conservative political activist James O'Keefe of Project Veritas.

Pointers for Evaluating News Validity

You have the power to discern fact from fiction and reject false and misleading content presented as legitimate news. Fake news content comes in print, broadcast, and digital forms. If a news story's headline evokes a strong "Whoa!" reaction, by making you extremely angry or sad, or by making you laugh out loud, this should be a red flag. Whether negative or positive, emotions could cloud your ability to think logically and objectively. As Allison Butler of the University of Massachusetts, Amherst (and one of this book's authors), reminds us, critically news-literate media users strive to cast themselves as "media citizens," rather than as "media consumers." They aim to identify truth to serve democracy, not to confirm their beliefs. You can do this by asking the following questions about news content:

☐ **Is the content journalism?** Not everyone in the press is a journalist. Commentators and pundits, such as Rachel Maddow of MSNBC, Sean Hannity of Fox News Channel, and Bakari Sellers of CNN, comment on news stories that other journalists originally reported. These commentators or pundits are rarely onsite for the story, in real time or afterward, and are less likely to have been involved in primary-source reporting. Another example, television news anchors often read what others have reported, but may not have been involved in the act of investigative reporting. By contrast, reporters and journalists generally introduce primary sources, explaining the known and verified events on a timeline while providing further context. They tell audiences what the available primary sources mean when analyzed together.

Media citizens determine whether the content was produced by a journalist or another source, such as a critic, commentator, or pundit. This determination is made by investigating whether the content serves the democratic functions of the press, follows valid criteria for determining genuine newsworthiness, and has been reported by an organization or individual that follows a journalistic code of ethics.

- **Who is the publisher of this content?** Evaluate the publisher's validity. This easy step can be taken early in the process of news evaluation. News users should consider the following questions: Does the publisher have a history of publishing fact-based journalism or biased content? Does the publisher have any conflicts of interest (economic, political, professional, or personal)? Do they have a history of retracting and correcting inaccurate reporting? Sometimes these questions can be answered by examining the "About" page, if the news organization has a website. Digging deeper, media analysts and watchdogs like Project Censored and Fairness & Accuracy in Reporting routinely report on such matters, calling attention to conflicts of interest.

▣ **Who is the author of this content?** Evaluate the author's credibility, another crucial early step. News users should consider the following questions: Who is the author? Does the author have any professional, personal, or political conflicts of interest? Do they have a history of having their stories retracted for inaccurate reporting?

▣ **Do I understand the content?** Slow down and carefully investigate content. Being well informed is *not* about virtue signaling or showing that you can share more articles online than any of your peers; it is about finding the truth, and that takes time. So spending more time with less content provides an opportunity to put your critical-thinking skills to work by examining the factual evidence and claims made in the news stories with which you engage.

▣ **What is the evidence?** Identify, evaluate, and analyze the evidence. Are the news story's sources clearly identified or not? Are there other newsworthy views or sources that ought to be included? Journalists sometimes have to use anonymous sources to protect the identity of vulnerable individuals and **whistleblowers**. For example, if a source is providing information about corruption in their workplace or within the government, they could be fired by their employer for doing so or, worse yet, charged with a crime and imprisoned. And at a legitimate news organization, an editor will look for independent verification of the facts before publishing. However, there can also be problems when journalists rely on anonymous sources, because the claims made by such sources can be difficult if not impossible to verify. As John Christie from the Poynter Institute notes, "That's one problem with anonymous sources: They often get it wrong because why make sure you [the journalist] have it right when you will not be held accountable for what you say. And even if it is accurate, readers cannot judge the value of the material for themselves if they don't know the source."[123]

It is a good idea to be skeptical of anonymous sources, but it is also important to note that at times anonymous sources have been remarkably significant. For example, two of the most famous news stories in the history of US journalism relied on anonymous sources: the revelations of the My Lai massacre in Vietnam and the Watergate scandal that eventually brought down President Richard Nixon's administration. This is another reason why protecting journalists and their sources is important. It also highlights how we count on journalists to make ethical choices when they use anonymous sources.

- ☐ **What is missing from the content?** Analyze news media not just for what is there but for what is missing. What stories and whose viewpoints are excluded? What identity groups are erased or marginalized, either as newsworthy sources of information and perspective or as journalists? What do these missing people and perspectives reveal about the aims and the validity of the news content? How do these missing perspectives reinforce or extend existing power relations?

▫ **What is the bias?** Identify and examine the influence of bias on news content. As we've mentioned, all content will have some bias, originating from a variety of sources. In addition to the political bias discussed in this chapter, AllSides, an online organization that analyzes and categorizes media bias, points out that there are ideological biases that go beyond partisan commitments to political parties. We have seen some of those at work in the creation of consumer culture, for example, as discussed in chapter 6. Corporate news coverage often reflects the values of consumer culture by emphasizing the interests of business owners, while ignoring the lives of working people.[124]

What Can You Do?

Critically media-literate citizens set themselves apart because they engage with content ready to ask questions and investigate rather than be passively informed. They recognize that news content is a resource that helps inform and shape our understanding of the world. It is important and influential, not something that should be simply shared and liked without consideration of its validity and accuracy.

CHAPTER 8

What Do You Want to Do?

A RESOURCE GUIDE

The Gears in the Clock: What's Next?

So you've read about critical thinking, media's impact on socialization and our sense of self and identity, critical media literacy, representation, multiple literacies, advertising and consumerism, and news. Now you can see the gears inside the clock, and you know more about how they work. Sometimes, when we get to new understandings, we want to *act on them*. We get excited and inspired and want to contribute to positive action. We want to change the things that frustrate us, that make us mad, that hurt us, our friends, other humans, and our world. And, inspired by heroic role models (who are not necessarily superheroes) and their accomplishments, we want to make positive contributions of our own. At this point, you might be asking yourself, "So how do I *do* that? I'm just one person. What can *I* do?"

The world is full of challenges—and opportunities to make active choices that can empower yourself and others. When it comes to media use, you can choose to be a *consumer*; you can also make decisions that render you the *product* being bought and sold. Our goal with *The Media and Me* has been to help you become a media citizen, and not just a consumer or a product. As you'll recall from chapter 1, a **media citizen** accesses, analyzes, evaluates, creates, and acts with media to empower themselves and others. Here we offer the acronym MEDIA AND ME, comprising ten guiding strategies for using media and the lessons learned in this book.

1. Maneuver Like a Media Citizen

As we noted in chapter 1, the media can provide useful tools to empower citizens. However, we also showed some ways that the media serve as tools of oppression that disempower us and undermine democracy. Given all the ways that the media exert influence on us, how can we make choices that cast us as active participants, rather than passive lab rats? In part, this involves rethinking your relationship with the media. We encourage you to act not like a mindless consumer of media but as a media citizen, to see media as a tool that can empower your life and the lives of those around you. As a result, you can reflect on how you use media in order to evaluate who is using whom. The following nine strategies provide more detail and specific resources on how to do just that.

2. Engage with Media at a Slower Pace

A theme throughout this book is how media companies try to persuade consumers to feel that they must be using media all the time, and that it is normal to do so. We are not here to lecture you on the amount of time you spend with the media, but we think there are benefits to engaging with media at a slower pace.

Although you may hear a lot about young people (and adults) spending "too much" time with the media, it is reasonable to ask, "What is the 'right' amount?" If you can spend "too much" time with the media, is it also possible to spend "too little" time? We suggest you consider a different question: How might a media citizen best use their time? At the very least, critical media literacy will help you slow down to make sure that you are *engaging* the media at a pace that makes sense for you, rather than at a speed dictated by media producers or peer pressure.

Slowing down creates opportunities for critical reflection and meaningful engagement. Slowing down makes room to become more aware of clickbait headlines, worn-out stereotypes, and provocative images. This, in turn, may mean that you spend more time in critical analysis and become less likely to be stressed out by the time you invest in media use or duped by misleading content.

RESOURCES

Even the pioneering founder of virtual reality, the technology critic Jaron Lanier, has addressed the problematic spike in time spent online and social media use and addiction in his book *Ten Arguments for Deleting Your Social Media Accounts Right Now*. You can learn more online at http://www.jaronlanier.com/tenarguments.html. Lanier was also featured in the popular Netflix documentary *The Social Dilemma*, which addressed these challenges. See https://www.thesocialdilemma.com.

The computer scientist Cal Newport coined the phrase "digital minimalism." He argues that digital tools were introduced as an added bonus to make our lives more convenient, but rather than simplifying our lives, they can actually make things more complex and stressful. He contends that media users can achieve digital minimalism by adopting a philosophy known as *digital declutter*. The process involves stepping away from optional online activities for thirty days in order to reduce the risk of addiction that digital tools instill in media users. See more at https://www.calnewport.com/blog/2016/12/18/on-digital-minimalism/.

3. Defend Freedom of Expression as a Human Right

Freedom of expression—the ability to communicate what we believe and value, *as well as* the opportunity to hear and engage with diverse perspectives of others whose beliefs may differ from our own—is a fundamental human right, as affirmed in Article 19 of the Universal Declaration of Human Rights. But, as we noted in the introduction, asserting that the freedom of expression is an inalienable human right does not automatically make it so. Free speech rights require constant and vigilant protection. You can take action on behalf of human rights by defending freedom of expression.

Help others understand why free speech is important, even when it is sometimes unpopular or even offensive. Here are three basic reasons why a free society depends on freedom of expression:

1. Free speech affirms the dignity and value of each and every person by serving as a basic foundation for self-fulfillment.

2. Free speech is vital to the development of understanding and the search for truth.

3. Free speech is a cornerstone of democracy—without it, members of the public are more vulnerable to oppression and tyranny.

Defending freedom of expression includes understanding what censorship is and using your voice to oppose it. From YouTube, where algorithms enforce community standards that restrict controversial content, to school libraries, which sometimes ban books on the grounds of indecency, there are many opportunities to speak out against specific cases of censorship.

RESOURCES

The website for Article 19, a human rights organization dedicated to defending the freedom to speak and the freedom to know, includes content on equality and hate speech, protest, surveillance, digital rights, and more. Find more at https://www.article19.org/what-we-do/.

The Algorithmic Justice League uses art, storytelling, and research to examine how artificial intelligence systems restrict the free flow of information and perpetuate discrimination. Find more at https://www.ajl.org/.

The National Coalition Against Censorship has been opposing censorship and book bans for more than forty years. Its *Kids' Right to Read Action Kit* empowers young people (and their parents) to fight book censorship. Find more at https://www.ncac.org/resource/book-censorship-toolkit.

4. Increase the Amount of Valuable Content

Cut junk content from your media diet. Media citizens recognize that some media content has great value while other content has less to offer. With critical media literacy, you are empowered to determine the value of content for yourself, rather than depending on others (such as a government, corporation, or school) to filter content for you.

Media citizens recognize that they have the power and the critical-thinking skills necessary to determine the value of content for themselves. That determination could be based on a desire to laugh and be entertained, or to learn more about what is going on in the world. Whatever the case may be, a media citizen chooses content that they value. They do not depend upon streaming services or news feeds to tell them what media they should be using. Rather, they investigate, analyze, and evaluate media content to determine what content is best for them. Of course, critical media literacy can also inform how you interpret that content.

RESOURCES

For cutting junk out of your news diet, see the documentary film *Project Censored the Movie: Ending the Reign of Junk Food News* (Hole in the Media Productions, 2013) online at http://www.projectcensoredthemovie.com or at Project Censored's YouTube channel.

For cutting junk out of your entertainment diet—the author Tiffany Shlain coordinated with her husband and two teenage children to turn off all their devices, together, for twenty-four hours each week. Shlain's book, *24/6: The Power of Unplugging One Day a Week*, and other resources and links are available at her website: https://www.tiffanyshlain.com/.

5. Acknowledge the Context

One way to assess the value of the content is to look at the context in which it was created. This involves investigating the background of the media producers. Who is writing this essay, hosting this radio show, or constructing this broadcast? Thinking back to chapter 1, you can begin to question the decisions that media producers made in how the content was constructed and delivered. With this background, you will have a better understanding of what that text is about and its intended purpose. For example, does it exist to make you laugh? Is it trying to make you upset about an event or person? If we focus solely on the content of the media, we risk missing how the *context* shapes that *content*.

RESOURCES

The Propwatch Project, introduced in chapter 5, exposes how basic propaganda techniques work. Its website features a dynamic video library of propaganda techniques, allowing visitors to view and identify actual examples of stealthy techniques at work in the real world. Find more at https://www.propwatch.org/.

The Propaganda Critic website equips citizens with tools for analyzing propaganda that can be used to defend against media manipulation, including how to decode propaganda and fight back against fake news. Find more at https://www.propagandacritic.com/.

6. Analyze Representation

Using critical media literacy helps to clarify how an understanding of the context is deepened by analysis of representation. As discussed in chapter 4, identities are expressions of power. The identities that are privileged to make media, and how they in turn represent other identities, reveals how power shapes media content. Tracking representation involves considering how racism, sexism, homophobia, ableism, and other forms of oppression are normalized and validated in media content.

Who is treated as worthy? Why is it that media representations typically center those with privilege, power, and wealth and either marginalize or erase those who are underprivileged, vulnerable, and poor? A critically media-literate citizen not only considers these patterns and practices but also questions what they reveal about the power dynamics that shape our society, including its means of production.

RESOURCES

The Critical Media Project provides tools for students and teachers interested in decoding media representations of race and ethnicity, gender and sexuality, class, religion, age, and disability. Its website empowers students to tell their own stories and create their own representations. Find more at https://www.criticalmediaproject.org.

ColorLines highlights news, art, and culture with a focus on race and ethnicity. Find more at https://www.colorlines.com.

The Media Education Foundation (MEF) produces and distributes documentary movies that address media representations of gender and sexuality, race, and class. Find MEF's extensive collection of films at https://www.mediaed.org/.

7. Never Forget the Means of Production

Context is shaped by the means of production, as discussed in chapter 3. One way to identify and understand the means of production is to "follow the money." Investigate who owns the media that you use and who sponsors the content you engage. For example, corporate news is driven by advertising and subscription revenue, and is shaped by the consolidation of corporate ownership. For the news you read or watch, ask: What economic interests shape this content?

Look for conflicts of interest that may limit or shape media narratives. For example, efforts to combat climate change threaten the profits of the fossil fuel industry. Be alert for (and perhaps wary of) any media content about climate change that is funded by the fossil fuel industry or that features "experts" (including scientists) sponsored by it.

RESOURCES

The *Columbia Journalism Review* maintains a database of media ownership that is useful for tracking who owns what and how different media companies are connected to one another. Find more at https://beta.cjr.org/resources/.

The DeSmog Blog features reporting on how the fossil fuel industry attempts to discredit the science on climate change. Find more at https://www.desmog.com/topic/science-denial/.

PR Watch: Center for Media and Democracy is a watchdog organization that calls out conflicts of interest, misleading claims, and flat-out falsehoods in messaging from corporations and government agencies. Find more at https://www.prwatch.org/cmd.

UnKoch My Campus is a student-driven organization

that investigates how big money donors, such as Charles and David Koch (the Koch brothers), use their wealth to promote corporate interests on college and university campuses. Find more at https://www.unkochmycampus.org/.

8. Draw On Independent Media Sources

Employ your ability to understand content in context and your knowledge about the forces of production to identify media sources that are independent of corporate funding. Independent sources are not primarily motivated by profit, though that does not ensure that they do not have biases or agendas of their own.

From music and movies to comics and news, independent versions of your favorite media exist. But they're often harder to find, because they do not enjoy the same prominence online as their corporate counterparts, due to real differences in advertising budgets, for example, and the ways that algorithms steer search optimization towards well-financed and biased content.

9. Make Solutions-Based Journalism a Priority

Media citizens seek out not only independent media but also independent sources that highlight solutions to everyday social problems.

As educators, we often hear from students who say they

do not pay attention to the news, because it is too negative and depressing. This is often the case, as studies show that corporate news media privilege stories that play on our fears, because doing so is profitable. It does not have to be that way.

The news and information that we media citizens need in order to fulfill our duties and our potential—as family members, community members, and citizens—include not only stories of power and its abuses but also examples of positive human actions, relationships, and institutions that are undergirded by first principles that bring out their very best.

RESOURCES

YES! Magazine publishes solutions journalism daily online and in a beautifully illustrated quarterly print magazine. Find more at https://www.yesmagazine.org/.

The Solutions Journalism Network's Solutions Story Tracker brings together positive news stories from diverse sources around the world. Find more at https://www.solutionsjournalism.org/storytracker.

10. Engage in Activism, not Slacktivism

Media citizens want to spot problematic content or familiarize themselves with independent and solutions-based media, but they also aim to *use* content to transform the world. Media are crucial tools that can help us become better informed and organized, but change does not occur based on how many online petitions you sign or what kind of online content you "like." Because these kinds of actions have little effect other than to make the individual doing them feel virtuous, this type of engagement is sometimes referred to as "slacktivism."

Real change is more likely to happen when media citizens use media to help organize communities and their members. Then media can amplify a movement's message and multiply its power.

Acting together, members of a movement can exert influence on powerful people and institutions. Using media to grow movements involves building awareness, sharing tools and concepts, organizing online, *and* taking that knowledge and organization off our devices, out of the classroom, and into the real world, where it can inform and inspire protests, civil disobedience, and campaigns that pressure those in power. Acting together, rather than as isolated individuals, we generate the influence necessary to hold powerful people accountable for their behavior and to transform social institutions that perpetuate discrimination and inequality.

Using a distinction between "platforms" and "pedestals," Alicia Garza (who helped found Black Lives Matter) describes how media attention can either empower or undermine movements for social change. Read a short excerpt from her book *The Purpose of Power* here: https://inthesetimes.com/article/black-lives-matter-organizing-movement-building.

Mari Copeny (Little Miss Flint) brought national and international attention to the water crisis in Flint, Michigan, using social media as her primary tool. She then took the work offline, helping to organize water bottle drives and other direct-assistance ventures. She has a number of suggestions for young activists: https://mashable.com/article/little-miss-flint-mari-copeny-how-to-be-a-young-activist. These are mostly about the importance of self-care, but we all need such lessons if we want to participate in activism without burning ourselves out.

What Else Can You Do? Engaging in Constructive Dialogue

If you put your critical media literacy skills to use, it will not be long before you encounter others who disagree with you. They may not share your commitment to critical thinking. When this happens, it helps to know how to engage in constructive dialogue. And even when we are largely in agreement with others, *how* we communicate can be as important as *what* we communicate. Details such as tone of voice and word choice impact how others hear what you have to say. It's important to focus on *constructive* dialogue.

Constructive dialogue aims to build trust and understanding.[125] This is achieved through clarity (making your message easy to follow), reciprocity (allowing space for give and take), and empathy (understanding how someone else feels based on their situation and experiences).

Constructive dialogue also hinges on *active listening*. Often we do not really listen in order to understand someone; instead, we're just waiting for our turn to speak. Before we engage in criticism or disagreement, the philosopher Daniel Dennett suggests the following steps:

1. Attempt to restate the other person's position, so clearly and fairly that the other person might say, *Thanks, I wish I'd thought of putting it that way.*

2. Identify any points of agreement you share with others in the conversation (especially if those points are not matters of general or widespread agreement).

3. Highlight anything you have learned from what others in the conversation have said.[126]

When dialogue is difficult, it can also help to:

- ☐ Clarify what kind of evidence might help the other person consider a change of mind;

- ☐ Suggest a "time out" so that each person can seek the best evidence to support their perspective; and

- ☐ Seek common ground to serve as the foundation for determining the roots of a disagreement.[127]

These skills can help keep a difficult conversation going. They can even help us learn how to "agree to disagree," so that we can continue to build our knowledge and enjoy better, more constructive communication with others.

Time to Practice What We Teach

We started this book by looking behind the surface of the clockface. We all know how to tell time—but most of us do not understand much about how clocks work. Much of this book has been concerned with the workings of the clock. Using that metaphor, our chapters have focused on the levers and gears, or the digital pulses, and the ways those levers, gears, and pulses operate beneath the surface.

We have asked you to reexamine a skill you know well—using media—in order to explore that action in a different way. We have asked you to make the *familiar unfamiliar* as a way to understand it better. Metaphorically, we have asked you to pause your mastery of telling time in order to understand better how the clock works. To do so, we shared a lot of terms and techniques to help you better understand your media environment.

Let's return to the surface, the clockface itself. We are not asking you to stop engaging with your media of choice. Rather, we want you to be able to enjoy the media *and* have a more multidimensional understanding of how they work.

At the beginning of this book, we wrote that "learning to tell time was all about understanding the relationship between the clock's hands and numbers." By this point in your reading, we hope you've learned more about the media than you knew before picking up this book. We hope you know more about the relationship between the clock's hands and its numbers, not to mention how the gears and springs beneath the surface affect how the clock works.

In addition to finding great joy and pleasure in your media use, we hope you have also found some new things to think about. Now, perhaps, you can enjoy your favorite song *and* understand how it was produced and how others might interpret it. Maybe you will continue to scroll through your social media feed *and* understand the construction of the algorithm that brought those images and stories directly to you. Perhaps now you will read a headline *and* recognize how it is working to grab your attention so that you will read the full article (and, by extension, stick around to read more articles and also see a lot of advertisements). Maybe you will decide that you want to add more news to your daily media diet—or maybe you want to take a break from the news so that you can employ some critical distance, as a way to understand it better when you return. You now have the opportunity to make your own media choices *and* possess a richer, more nuanced background knowledge of those choices.

Our clocks will continue to tick forward and media will continue to expand. Thank you for taking this journey with us. We hope it provides you with a solid foundation for understanding the media, an omnipresent and powerful aspect of the world we all share.

Glossary

Abductive inference: An inference that relies on the certainty of a major premise, and the probability of smaller premises to draw a conclusion.

Access: The state of being able to use media tools and content.

Action economy: An economy in which companies operationalize users' data to direct rather than predict those users' behavior.

Ad hominem: A fallacy attacking a person or the source of an argument rather than addressing the argument being made.

Algorithm: A design process, a set of rules, within digital media; a way to organize data.

Algorithmic literacy: The ability to recognize biases in computer programming that affect the availability of information online, as well as to understand how the use of digital platforms involves sacrifices in privacy.

Appeal to authority: The fallacy of believing claims because an alleged expert is cited in argument.

Appeal to emotion: The fallacy of exploiting emotional feelings to build support for an argument.

Appeal to ignorance: The fallacy of preying on one's lack of knowledge regarding a particular topic.

Argument: A claim that leads to a conclusion, based on a series of inferences supported by evidence.

Attention economy: An economy in which businesses, especially media and technology companies, compete for the attention of consumers.

Aural literacy: The ability to analyze, interpret, and negotiate the meaning of sound.

Bandwagon / ad populum: The fallacy of believing something is true because a majority of people agree.

Begging the question / circular reasoning: The fallacy of restating the premise as conclusion without evidence.

Belief: A conviction based on something other than evidence, such as faith, morals, or values.

Bias: An individual's preference or prejudice. Compare with **slant**.

Binary thinking: Oversimplified thinking where multiple options are reduced to only two, usually one good and one bad; see also **false dilemma** fallacy.

Brandalism: "Vandalizing" brands or images that are key to a corporation's success in order to create alternative, anti-consumerist messaging.

Branding: Forming identity for a company *through* the way it present its products to the buying public.

Brand loyalty: Customer preference for a particular brand (company) or product (over other products offered by competing companies), usually created by emotional connections produced through marketing rather than on the basis of the brand or product's quality.

Celebratory media literacy: The position that most media are generally good and that young people's active interaction with media is positive.

Censorship: The suppression of speech, public communication, or other information on the grounds that it is objectionable, harmful, or sensitive.

Cherry-picking: The process of suppressing facts that oppose or undermine one's position, while emphasizing only those facts that support one's position.

Cisgender: When a person's gender identity or gender expression aligns with the sex assigned at birth.

Claim: An assertion of truth that is typically disputed or in doubt. Strong claims offer qualifiers and exceptions.

Cognitive bias: A prejudice or inclination that shapes a person's reasoning.

Cognitive dissonance: When one encounters information that contradicts one's preexisting beliefs or ideas about a certain matter or topic.

Confirmation bias: The tendency to search for, interpret, and favor information that reinforces or supports one's values or prior beliefs.

Conglomeration: The process by which a single corporation acquires ownership of a variety of otherwise unrelated businesses. Sometimes also referred to as consolidation or concentration of ownership.

Consumer culture: A culture in which money and behaviors revolve around consumption.

Consumerism: The attachment to material goods and the belief that problems can be solved through purchasing or otherwise acquiring goods and services.

Conventions: Shared ideas and understandings that allow for cooperative activity. Also referred to as "customs" or "norms," conventions reduce the need to negotiate how to do something in each new situation.

Correlation fallacy: The fallacy that correlation implies causation. Expressed in Latin: *Cum hoc, post hoc, ergo propter hoc.*

Critically media-literate citizen: A person who accesses, analyzes, evaluates, creates, and acts with media to empower their life and the lives of those around them.

Critical thinking: General strategies that might be used in a variety of problem situations to gather and evaluate data, generate hypotheses, assess evidence, and arrive at conclusions.

Culture jamming: Manipulating existing advertising or marketing images and text in order to critique not only mass media messaging but the corporate agenda and underlying structures behind such messages; also known as **subvertising**.

Curse-of-knowledge bias: When an individual assumes that everyone should know what they know.

Data: Information collected through research. Facts or statistics, records of observations that are used to make interpretations. The plural of "datum."

Declinism bias: The contention that the past was better than the present.

Deductive inference: A inference that assumes that because the premise is true, then so is the conclusion.

Deep fakes: Fraudulent videos that appear real, but are in fact a kind of synthetic media in which the image of a person is blended with or replaced by another.

Digital literacy: See **algorithmic literacy**.

Digital redlining: The practice of creating and perpetuating inequalities among already marginalized groups through the use of digital technologies, digital content, and the internet. See also **redlining**.

Disinformation: Messages intended to be false or misleading.

Dissonance reduction: The process by which biases work to alleviate cognitive dissonance.

Dunning-Kruger effect: When people with more knowledge about a topic act with caution when discussing the topic to give the impression that they know less than they do, while those with less knowledge treat the topic as simplistic, acting as if they have more knowledge than they actually do.

Emotional transfer: A process by which advertisers foster positive emotions in viewers, through the "plot" or situations of the ad, and then transfer those emotions to the product or brand.

Encoding-decoding model: A media theory that treats the meaning of a media message as a negotiated combination of both the meaning intended by the message's creator (encoding) and the interpretations made by the message's audiences (decoding). The encoding-decoding model challenges the assumption that audiences passively accept whatever meanings were intended by the message's creator.

Evidence: The known facts and information available to test a claim.

Fact: Verifiable information.

Fallacy: A faulty or inaccurate claim. Fallacies can involve either unintentional errors in reasoning or deliberate misinformation intended to cajole or trick people.

False analogy: A fallacy comparing unlike things as though they were more related than they are.

False dilemma: A fallacy forcing an option between two choices when there are more.

Filter bubble: An environment, especially online, in which people are exposed only to opinions and information that conform to their existing beliefs.

Forer effect: The practice of personalizing vague information, making it specific to one's self without consideration of the fact that it could be applied to anyone and could have many different interpretations from the one accepted by the individual. Also known as the [P. T.] Barnum effect.

Fourth estate: A term for the **press** that highlights its function as an informal fourth branch of the government (after the executive, legislative, and judiciary) that serves as another of the checks and balances on power.

Framing: The organization of experience or attention to include some matters while excluding or marginalizing others. Based on the idea of a window or a picture frame, the concept of framing comprises the practices used by media texts to direct the audience's attention.

Halo effect: The fallacy of assigning positive attributes to a source based on one issue or situation.

Hasty generalization: A fallacy based on jumping to a conclusion after only cursory observation.

Hegemonic: Having dominant control over individuals or society; from "hegemony," which means leadership or control over a group of individuals *with their consent*. Put another way, it is the manufacture of consent.

Hindsight bias: When individuals claim that an outcome was obvious, because they know what happened.

Hypodermic needle theory: A theory of media effects that treats the audience as passive recipients of the meanings intended by a message's creator. In this view, the audience is powerless to resist the message creator's influence. For contrast, see **encoding-decoding model**.

Ideology: A system of beliefs, attitudes, and values that tend to reproduce the existing social order, including what is considered right and wrong, as well as which groups are perceived to be powerful, famous, and respected, and which groups are not.

Inductive inference: Drawing conclusions by going from specifics to generalizations.

Inference: A reasoning step that generates a conclusion based on available information.

Inferred justification: When a person assumes there must be a reason or reasons that a particular event has taken place.

In-group: A group that one identifies with and feels loyalty toward.

In-group bias: When an individual displays a tendency to say favorable things about a person based solely on the fact that they belong to the same group.

Interpretive communities: Groups of people whose shared values, beliefs, and assumptions lead them to make sense of the world in similar ways.

Intersectionality: A concept that highlights how different categories of inequality (including, for example, race, gender, and class) overlap and interconnect to explain historic, systemic oppression and discrimination.

Inverted pyramid: A news **convention** characterized by reporting the most important, essential facts about a news story first, including who did what, and when, where, and why they did it.

Knowledge: The facts, information, and skills acquired through experience or education that provide theoretical or practical understanding of a subject.

Legacy media: Pre-digital-era media outlets, such as print newspapers and network television stations.

Liberatory: Something that is liberating; from "liberty," the condition of being free from oppressive restriction or control.

Linguistic profiling: The process of analyzing an individual's speech or writing in an attempt to identify or characterize an aspect of someone's identity.

Linguistic representation: The way that different languages, dialects, accents, and speech patterns are presented or omitted in media.

Linguistic stereotyping: Making assumptions about someone's characteristics or beliefs based on language usage and accent.

Literacy: At its most foundational level, the ability to read, write, and comprehend the written word. Increasingly, however, the term has been expanded to refer to the ability to interpret and express meaning in other forms. Thus, critical media literacy, the focus of this book, refers to the ability to critically analyze media messages and how they are produced.

Logic: The process and assessment of reasoning in accordance with strict principles of validity.

Looking-glass self: The notion, introduced by Charles Cooley, that the self develops through our perceptions of others' evaluations and appraisals of us.

Meaning: The idea conveyed or intended to be conveyed by language, image, or action.

Means of production: Generally, the raw materials, tools, and human labor employed in the production process. For media, the means of production can be specified in terms of the ownership of media outlets and platforms, the division of labor between media producers and media consumers, and how the text or content came to be; see also **political economy**.

Media: Channels of communication; alternately, "the media," the powerful institutions that control those channels and our access to them.

Media buy: The purchase of advertising from a media company.

Media citizen: See **critically media-literate citizen**.

Media multitasking: Using more than one tool or technology simultaneously.

Medium: A channel of information, a way to convey information. See **media**.

Metamessaging: A form of **paralinguistic communication** that includes how a speaker conveys intent beyond what is actually stated. Metamessaging indicates how a speaker intends their words to be interpreted in context.

Metaverse: A virtual world, characterized by immersive online experience using augmented reality and virtual reality, in which people work, play, and socialize.

Misinformation: False or misleading messages, possibly unintentional.

Motivated reasoning: Individuals' tendency to consider and evaluate evidence in a way that allows only for their preferred conclusion.

Objectivity: In critical thinking, impartial and balanced thinking about the evidence. In journalism, a goal of reporting, also based on impartial, balanced coverage.

Opinion: As used in critical thinking, an attempt to draw an honest judgment based upon the facts.

Optimism bias: When individuals' predictions about a positive outcome reflect the positive feelings they have at that particular moment.

Out-group: A group toward which one feels opposition, rivalry, or hostility.

Paralinguistic communication: Messages conveyed during conversations that can be understood outside the words themselves. This includes gestures, tone, images, and more. Also see **metamessaging**.

Pessimism bias: When individuals' predictions about a

negative outcome reflect the negative feelings they have at that particular moment.

Political economy: A form of analysis focused on the ownership, production, and distribution of goods and services.

Political party propaganda apparatuses: A loosely connected group of actors who work to shape electoral outcomes and policy debates through the use of content including fake news.

Post-truth: relating to or denoting circumstances in which objective facts are less influential than appeals to emotion and personal belief in shaping public opinion.

Predictive analytic products: Data analysis that anticipates a user's response or behavior at a particular moment, soon thereafter, and even much later; data that is operationalized for companies to microtarget a particular individual or group with effective messaging.

Press: Journalists and news outlets.

Primary source: A point of origin, such as an eyewitness account or original historic document.

Production of discontent: In advertising, the creation

of dissatisfaction in oneself, including, for example, the premise that there is something wrong with you, some flaw that can be solved only by buying and using a promoted product.

Propaganda: A systematic and intentional form of persuasion that aims to influence the emotions, attitudes, opinions, and actions of a target audience for ideological, political, or commercial purposes. Propaganda works through controlled transmission of one-sided messages (which may or may not be factual) via mass- and direct-media channels.

Protectionist: The position that argues the media are generally bad and young people should be taught to stay away from them.

Pseudoscience: A process that is discordant with the scientific method, and produces non-replicable results based on opinions, beliefs, or practices that are introduced as facts.

Qualifier: A word or phrase that modifies how certain, absolute, or generalizable a statement is.

Reasoning: A set of processes and abilities that act as a problem-solving tool.

Red herring: An argument not relevant to the issue. Something that misleads or distracts from the topic or question at hand.

Redlining: The discriminatory practice of outlining neighborhoods and communities where banks would avoid investments based on community demographics. Critical scholars including Safiya Umoja Noble have adapted the term to describe discriminatory digital practices; see **digital redlining**.

Representation: Literally to re-present. The way that images or text *reconstruct*, rather than simply *reflect*, the original sources that they depict. Sometimes used more specifically to refer to whether and how media portray specific types of people or communities.

Satirical fake news: A form of entertainment that lampoons dominant culture by simulating a major news outlet's format and presentation.

Secondary source: From somewhere other than the original, such as someone repeating what they heard from an eyewitness or commenting about a primary-sourced event.

Self-serving bias: The practice in which individuals attribute positive outcomes to their own behavior and negative outcomes to others.

Slant: The persistent framing of news reports and editorials to favor one side over others, indicating how news media may *systematically* help distribute power to particular groups, causes, or individuals. Compare with **bias**.

Slippery slope: The fallacy of claiming that because one negative thing may occur others will surely follow.

Social construct: An idea that has been created and accepted in society.

Social media: Applications and websites that allow users to create, interact, and participate with one another in ways that work like a community.

Socialization: The lifelong process by which we become members of a group, which involves learning the group's values and beliefs. Family, peers, school, and the media are four basic agents of socialization.

Spin: A twist put on a story that aims to influence the audience's interpretation.

Sponsored content: Also known as "sponcon," content in a media message that is paid for by a manufacturer or advertiser; sponcon often takes the form of messages from social media influencers.

State-sponsored propaganda machines: A conglomerate of government-funded efforts that seek to influence public opinion.

Stereotype: A judgment based on preconceived generalizations about a group or category of people.

Straw person: A fallacy involving the distortion of an argument or position so that it is easier to dismiss.

Subjective thinking: Reaching a conclusion based on one's personal feelings and preferences.

Substitution effect: The replacement of other activities by media consumption, often with negative effects for the user.

Subtweeting: The practice of making a post or comment directed toward or in reference to someone without tagging them or sending it directly to them.

Subvertising: See **culture jamming**.

Sweeping generalization: The fallacy of casting inclusive categorization instead of recognizing complexity and diversity.

Symbol: Any act or object that represents an idea or concept. Symbols are usually open to multiple, potentially conflicting meanings.

Tertiary source: A thirdhand source, one that collates and summarizes primary and secondary sources, such as a textbook.

Unconscious or implicit bias: The process by which a person unknowingly uses assumptions about individuals and groups to draw a conclusion about them.

Validity: The condition of being sound or genuine. A measure of the extent to which a claim, a concept, or a measure corresponds accurately to the real world.

Visual literacy: The ability to analyze, interpret, and negotiate the meaning of imagery in television, movies, gaming, and news.

Whistleblower: A person who discloses information about abuse, corruption, or dangers to public health and safety that otherwise would not be known.

Wishful thinking: Convincing oneself that something is true, regardless of what the evidence suggests, simply because one wants it to be true.

Deeper Reading

The following books, articles, and websites expand on the ideas and examples presented in *The Media and Me*. If you want to go deeper into some of the topics this book has introduced, these sources will take you there. Most of the titles listed below were written for adults. You may find them to be more challenging to read than this book. But we recommend these sources confident that *The Media and Me* has prepared you to meet those challenges.

Adbusters, https://www.adbusters.org.

Mark Brilliant, "Research & Writing Guide," Department of History, University of California Berkeley, accessed August 9, 2021, https://history.berkeley.edu/undergraduate/academic-resources/research-writing-guide.

M. Neil Browne and Stuart M. Keeley, *Asking the Right Questions: A Guide to Critical Thinking*, Twelfth Edition (New York: Pearson, 2018).

David Croteau and William Hoynes, *Media/Society: Industries, Images, and Audiences* (Thousand Oaks, CA: Sage Publications, 2014).

Daniel C. Dennett, *Intuition Pumps and Other Tools for Thinking* (New York: W. W. Norton & Company, 2013).

Jennifer L. Eberhardt, *Biased: Uncovering the Hidden Prejudice That Shapes What We See, Think, and Do* (New York: Viking, 2018).

Virginia Eubanks, *Automating Inequality: How High-Tech Tools Profile, Police, and Punish the Poor* (New York: St. Martin's Press, 2017).

"The Fallacy Files Taxonomy of Logical Fallacies," Fallacy Files, accessed May 25, 2022, https://www.fallacyfiles.org/taxonnew.htm.

Stuart Hall, "Encoding/Decoding," in *Culture, Media, Language*, eds. Stuart Hall, Dorothy Hobson, Andrew Lowe, and Paul Tillis (London: Hutchinson, 1980), 128–38.

Chris Hedges, *War Is a Force That Gives Us Meaning* (New York: Public Affairs, 2002).

Edward Herman and Noam Chomsky, *Manufacturing Con-*

sent: The Political Economy of the Mass Media (New York: Pantheon Books, 1988).

Nolan Higdon and Mickey Huff, *United States of Distraction: Media Manipulation in Post-Truth America (And What We Can Do About It)* (San Francisco: City Lights Books, 2019).

Nolan Higdon and Mickey Huff, *Let's Agree to Disagree: A Critical Thinking Guide to Communication, Conflict Management, and Critical Media Literacy* (New York and London: Routledge, 2022).

Mickey Huff and Andy Lee Roth, ed., *Project Censored's State of the Free Press 2023* (New York and Fair Oaks: Seven Stories Press and The Censored Press, 2022). **Note:** When *The Media and Me* was first published, *State of the Free Press 2022* was the most recent volume of Project Censored's yearbook. More up-to-date editions of *State of the Free Press* may now be available; previous editions of the yearbook, dating back to 1996, can be found at the Project Censored webpage on the Seven Stories Press website, https://www.sevenstories.com/authors/314-project-censored.

Jaron Lanier, *Ten Arguments for Deleting Your Social Media Account Right Now* (New York: Henry Holt, 2018).

Walter Lippmann, *Public Opinion* (New Brunswick, NJ, and London: Transaction Publishers, 1998[1922]).

Steve Macek and Andy Lee Roth, "It's True That Corporate Media Is Biased—But Not in the Ways Right-Wingers Say," Truthout, November 27, 2020, https://truthout.org/articles/its-true-that-corporate-media-is-biased-but-not-in-the-ways-right-wingers-say/.

"Manufacturing Consumers," *The Ad and the Ego*, dir. Harold Boihem (Burbank, CA: Parallax Pictures, 1997).

Lee McIntyre, *Post-Truth* (Cambridge, MA: The MIT Press, 2018).

Safiya Umoja Noble, *Algorithms of Oppression: How Search Engines Reinforce Racism* (New York: New York University Press, 2018).

Cathy O'Neil, *Weapons of Math Destruction: How Big Data Increases Inequality and Threatens Democracy* (New York: Broadway Books, 2016).

Eli Pariser, *The Filter Bubble: How the New Personalized Web Is Changing What We Read and How We Think* (New York: Penguin, 2011).

Peter Phillips, *Giants: The Global Power Elite* (New York: Seven Stories Press, 2018).

Purdue Online Writing Lab, "How to Write a Lead," Purdue University, accessed May 25, 2022, https://owl. purdue.edu/owl/subject_specific_writing/journalism_and_ journalistic_writing/writing_leads.html.

Andy Lee Roth, "The New Gatekeepers: How Proprietary Algorithms Increasingly Determine the News We See," The Markaz Review, March 15, 2021, https://themarkaz.org/ magazine/the-new-gatekeepers-andy-lee-roth.

Carl Sagan, *The Demon-Haunted World: Science as a Candle in the Dark* (New York: Random House, 1995).

Michael Schudson, *The Sociology of News* (New York: W. W. Norton & Company, 2003). See esp. Chapter 5, "The Politics of Narrative Form."

Tiffany Shlain, *24/6: The Power of Unplugging One Day a Week* (New York: Gallery Books, 2019).

The Social Dilemma, dir. Jeff Orlowski (Los Gatos, CA: Netflix, 2020).

Paul Starr, *The Creation of the Media: Political Origins of*

Modern Communications (New York: Basic, 2004).

UN General Assembly, "Universal Declaration of Human Rights," 217 (III) A (Paris, 1948), https://www.un.org/en/about-us/universal-declaration-of-human-rights.

Siva Vaidhyanathan, *Anti-Social Media: How Facebook Disconnects Us and Undermines Democracy* (New York: Oxford University Press, 2018).

Jacob E. Van Vleet, *Informal Logical Fallacies: A Brief Guide*, Revised Edition (Lanham, MD: Hamilton Books, 2021).

"What Is Modern Censorship?," Project Censored, accessed May 25, 2022, https://www.projectcensored.org/censorship/.

Tim Wu, *The Attention Merchants: The Epic Scramble to Get Inside Our Heads* (New York: Vintage Books, 2017).

Shoshana Zuboff, *The Age of Surveillance Capitalism: The Fight for the Future at the New Frontier of Power* (New York: Public Affairs, 2019).

Shoshanna Zuboff, "You Are Now Remotely Controlled," *New York Times*, January 24, 2020, https://www.nytimes.com/2020/01/24/opinion/sunday/surveillance-capitalism.html.

Acknowledgments

The Media Revolution Collectives gives thanks and praise
to Dan Simon, our editor, and Conor O'Brien, copy
editor, as well as the entire team at Seven Stories Press and
Triangle Square Books, including especially Jon Gilbert,
Claire Kelley, Tal Mancini, Ruth Weiner, Allison Paller, and
Anastasia Damaskou; Peter Glanting and Stewart Cauley
for cover art and design; the editorial board of the Cen-
sored Press, including Nora Barrows-Friedman, Mischa
Geracoulis, Mickey Huff, Veronica Santiago Liu, Andy Lee
Roth, Dan Simon, and T. M. Scruggs; and Lorna Garano
of Lorna Garano Book Publicity. The collective is also
grateful to James W. S. Allard, Ethan Holiday, and Opal
Wright, who read and commented on early drafts of *The
Media and Me*.

This is the second book to be jointly published by
Seven Stories Press and the Censored Press, the publishing
imprint of Project Censored. Special thanks to John and
Lyn Roth and T. M. Scruggs for their vision and support in
making the Censored Press a reality.

avram anderson would like to thank Izek, Ayden, Jaxon,

Beau, and Olivia—for their inspiration and priceless insight into the minds and worlds of young folx living in the digital era.

Ben Boyington would like to thank his wife, Carla, for her ready ear and quiet support; the Project Censored co-conspirators for inviting him on board; and his co-authors for their patience.

Allison Butler thanks the readers of the early drafts, especially Jasmin Butler, whose insight and commentary were invaluable to the process. Thanks to the Department of Communication, the College of Social and Behavioral Sciences, and the Alan & Carol LeBovidge Undergraduate Research Award at the University of Massachusetts Amherst for financial support, and Erica Scharrer for her continued moral support and friendship. And, as always, thanks to Andy and Addie for continued love and support on the home front.

Peter Glanting would like to give a special thanks to his momma and pop, Paul, Vivien, the Stickies, and Justin.

Nolan Higdon gives a big thank-you to all the misanthropes, contrarians, and gadflies who inspire us to practice self-reflection and critical inquiry.

Kate Horgan extends her endless appreciation for the wisdom, love, and support from her parents and sister. Gratitude for Robbie, her teacher and friend, for always inspiring her. A special thanks to Allison Butler for bringing her into this incredible project and introducing her to her fellow co-authors.

Mickey Huff would like to thank his students and fellow educators for all they do to make the world a better place by seeking and imparting knowledge. He's grateful to his family for their patience, counsel, understanding, and amazing support, especially his wife, Meg, without whom he would not be able to do this important work. He's blessed to have two critically thinking, media-savvy children, Molly and Micah, who help him understand media culture through different lenses. Finally, Mickey thanks all the co-authors who came together to create Project Censored and the Media Revolution Collective. For the Revolution!

Reina Robinson would like to give endless appreciation to the youth for their inspiration. Stay motivated by curiosity and creativity! Continue to question and challenge that which you sense is unjust. Long hugs and much love to her family for riding along on every adventure and reminding her of her purpose. "When the roots are deep, there is no reason to fear the wind."

Andy Lee Roth extends deep gratitude to all the teachers—in classrooms and beyond—who have encouraged him to "look beneath the surface"; to family, friends, and artists who remind him that each sunrise is a new beginning; and in loving memory of Sasha Black (2003–2022), challenger of the unknown.

Maria Cecilia Soto would like to extend all of her thanks and love to her family and friends for supporting her in all her endeavors, especially her parents, Miriam and Carlos Soto, for raising her to be a critical thinker, an attentive person, and teaching her to love academia. Also, with much appreciation to staff and faculty in UCSC's Merrill College, Applied Linguistics, and Linguistics departments for encouraging her to be inquisitive and to collaborate with others across differences. Thanks to the Project Censored Media Revolution Collective for inviting her to work on this project and to Nolan Higdon for teaching and guiding her through her first years of her college career.

About the Authors

avram anderson is an electronic resources management specialist in the university library at California State University, Northridge, and a member and advocate of the LGBTQI+ community researching LGBTQI+ censorship, in print and online. They are also a member of the Diversity, Equity, Inclusion, and Accessibility Leadership Committee at the National Information Standards Organization (NISO). Recent publications include "Queer Erasure" in the Spring 2020 issue of *Index on Censorship*; "Stonewalled: Establishment Media's Silence on the Trump Administration's Crusade against LGBTQ People," featured in *Censored 2020*; and, as co-editor, *A Call for Change: Minnesota Environmental Justice Heroes in Action* (2021).

Nicholas Baham III is a professor and chair in the Department of Ethnic Studies at California State University, East Bay. He is the author of *The Coltrane Church: Apostles of Sound, Agents of Social Justice*; the co-author of *The Podcaster's Dilemma: Decolonizing Podcasters in the Era of Surveillance Capitalism* with Nolan Higdon; and the co-editor and co-author of *Love, Knowledge, Revolution: A Comparative Ethnic Studies Reader*.

Ben Boyington is an advocate for integrating critical media literacy into K–12 schools, a high school educator, and the father of two teenagers who are immersed in the worlds of video games, Discord, and Twitch, as well as anime and other visual storytelling. (They also read books now and then, and occasionally join their parents for dinner.) A member of the Media Freedom Foundation board and the former vice president of the Action Coalition for Media Education, Ben designs and conducts teacher trainings with Mass Media Literacy, in partnership with Allison Butler and Nolan Higdon. In his daily life, he works with high school students on self-directed learning and builds student-centered programming for a rural high school in Vermont. An avid media consumer, with a particular interest in film and television, he also enjoys music and podcasts, but eschews video games because they have too many buttons now.

Allison Butler is a senior lecturer, the director of under-graduate advising, and the director of the Media Literacy Certificate Program in the Department of Communication at the University of Massachusetts, Amherst, where she teaches courses on critical media literacy and represen-tations of education in the media. Butler co-directs the grassroots organization Mass Media Literacy (www.mass-medialiteracy.org), where she develops and runs teacher trainings for the inclusion of critical media literacy in K–12 schools. She is on the board of Action Coalition for Media Education (ACME) and serves as the vice president of the board of the Media Freedom Foundation. She holds an MA and a PhD from New York University. She is the author of numerous articles and books on media literacy, most recently, *Educating Media Literacy: The Need for Teacher Education in Critical Media Literacy* (Brill, 2020) and *Key Scholarship in Media Literacy: David Buckingham* (Brill, 2021), and the co-author of *Critical Media Literacy and Civic Learning*, a critical media literacy accompaniment to the open-source social studies textbook *Building Democracy for All* (EdTech Books, 2021).

Peter Glanting is an illustrator and product designer. He also claims he was a baron in "the old country," but people are haters and they do not often believe him (#notfair). He likes sock puppets and dogs with bushy eyebrows. Peter holds a BA in English from the University of California at Davis, and an MFA in comics from the California College of the Arts. He lives and works in Portland, Oregon.

Nolan Higdon is an author and university lecturer of history and media studies. Higdon's areas of concentration include podcasting, digital culture, news media history, and critical media literacy. Higdon is a founding member of the Critical Media Literacy Conference of the Americas. He sits on the boards of the Action Coalition for Media Education (ACME) and Northwest Alliance for Alternative Media and Education. He is the author of *The Anatomy of Fake News: A Critical News Literacy Education* (University of California Press, 2020). His most recent publications include *The*

Podcaster's Dilemma: Decolonizing Podcasters in the Era of Surveillance Capitalism (Wiley, 2021) with Nicholas Baham III and *Let's Agree to Disagree: A Critical Thinking Guide to Communication, Conflict Management, and Critical Media Literacy* (Routledge, 2022) with Mickey Huff. He is a long-time contributor to the Project Censored yearbook series. In addition, he has been a contributor to Truthout and *CounterPunch*; and a source of expertise for the *New York Times, San Francisco Chronicle*, and numerous television news outlets.

Kate Horgan is an undergraduate student and researcher in the Commonwealth Honors College at the University of Massachusetts, Amherst, studying communication and psychology with a certificate in media literacy. Kate discovered her passion for media literacy during her time with the Center for Curriculum Redesign where she created motion graphics to teach critical thinking skills to K–12 learners. She currently works at UMass's radio station, WMUA 91.1 FM, as the news operator, orchestrating daily news broadcasts and audio features for their podcast, *Beats Per Minute*. Kate has previously assisted fellow author Allison Butler in pop culture research for the chapter "Judgment Based on Gender; Patriarchy as a Form of Censorship" in *Censorship, Digital Media and the Global Crackdown on Freedom of Expression*. When she is not catching up on the latest pop culture content, Kate enjoys crafting, gardening, and exploring the Pioneer Valley.

Mickey Huff is the director of Project Censored and president of the Media Freedom Foundation. To date, he has co-edited thirteen volumes of Project Censored's annual book series. He is co-author with Nolan Higdon of *United States of Distraction: Media Manipulation in Post-Truth America (And What We Can Do About It)* (City Lights Books, 2019) and *Let's Agree to Disagree: A Critical Thinking Guide to Communication, Conflict Management, and Critical Media Literacy* (Routledge, 2022). He is a professor of social science, history, and journalism at Diablo Valley College in the San Francisco Bay Area, where he is chair of the journalism department. In 2019, Huff received the Beverly Kees Educator Award as part of the James Madison Freedom of Information Award from the Society for Professional Journalists, Northern California. He is also the executive producer and host of *The Project Censored Show*, the weekly syndicated public affairs program that originates from KPFA Pacifica Radio in Berkeley, California, and which airs on more than fifty stations around the United States. He lives in Northern California with his family and two heavy metal pets, Lemmy the dog and Ozzy the cat.

Reina Robinson is a coordinator of services for San Francisco Bay Area justice-involved youth since 2016. She earned a BA in ethnic studies and Black studies, with a minor in genders and sexualities in communities of color, plus a master of arts degree in communication at California

State University, East Bay. Reina is a certified community resiliency model (CRM) and youth mental health first aid (YMHFA) instructor, vice-chair of the Museum of Children's Art, and founder of the Center for Urban Excellence, a nonprofit organization whose mission is to foster resilience in system-involved youth using education, and economic and social opportunities. She resides in her hometown of Vallejo, California, and designs events focusing on Black experiences, the future, mental health, and resilience. Outside her profession, she enjoys live music, hiking, BBQing with family, and reading Afrofuturism.

Andy Lee Roth serves as the associate director of Project Censored, a nonprofit news watch organization that opposes censorship and promotes critical media literacy. Studying sociology in college made him curious about the connections between social identity and power. Sociology also developed his lifelong fascination with different subcultures. He became interested in the power of news to shape our understanding of reality while pursuing a PhD in sociology at the University of California, Los Angeles. He enjoys running long distances and playing tabletop board games with friends and family. Born and bred in Southern California, he now lives in a rural town in north-central Washington state with his sweetheart, Liz, and their remarkable cat, Eddie.

Maria Cecilia Soto is an undergraduate student at the University of California, Santa Cruz, studying applied linguistics and linguistics with a concentration in Spanish and teaching English as a second language. They are a student leader on campus, working as a residential assistant, and have experience working in the university classroom as a course assistant for Merrill College's academic literacy and ethos course. Maria Cecilia is also involved in student life as one of the faces of UCSC's promotional campaigns on campus and online. They greatly enjoy dancing and reading in their spare time.

Notes

1. Kaiser Family Foundation, "Daily Media Use Among Children and Teens Up Dramatically From Five Years Ago," January 20, 2010.
2. Sam Wineberg, Sarah McGrew, Joel Breakstone, and Teresa Ortega, "Evaluating Information: The Cornerstone of Civic Online Reasoning," Stanford History Education Group, November 22, 2016.
3. Universal Declaration of Human Rights, General Assembly of the United Nations, 1948.
4. Charles Horton Cooley, *Human Nature and the Social Order* (New York: Charles Scribner's Sons, 1902), 152.
5. David Croteau and William Hoynes, *Media/Society: Industries, Images, and Audiences* (Thousand Oaks, CA: Sage Publications, 2014), 8.
6. Paul Starr, *The Creation of the Media: Political Origins of Modern Communications* (New York: Basic, 2004), xi.
7. Chip Scanlan, "Writing from the Top Down: Pros and Cons of the Inverted Pyramid," Poynter, June 20, 2003.
8. Michael Schudson, "The Politics of Narrative Form," in *The Sociology of News* (New York: W. W. Norton & Company, 2003), 67–8.
9. Carma Hassan, "This Is How Americans in 1865 Found Out President Lincoln Was Assassinated," CNN, April 11, 2019.
10. Schudson, "The Politics of Narrative Form."
11. Peter Phillips, *Giants: The Global Power Elite* (New York: Seven Stories Press, 2018).
12. Ryan Derousseau, "Apple Isn't the First to Hit $1 Trillion in Value. Here Are 5 Companies That Did It Earlier," *Money*, August 2, 2018.
13. Ibid.
14. Stuart Hall, "Encoding/Decoding," in *Culture, Media, Language*, eds. Stuart

Hall, Dorothy Hobson, Andrew Lowe, and Paul Tillis (London: Hutchinson, 1980), 128–38.

15. Robert K. Merton, *Social Theory and Social Structure* (New York: The Free Press, 1968).

16. Russell Smith, "The Impact of Hate Media in Rwanda," BBC News, December 3, 2003.

17. Ibid.

18. William Ferroggiaro, ed., "The US and the Genocide in Rwanda 1994: Evidence of Inaction," August 20, 2001. See, in particular, Document 10, Memorandum from Under Secretary of Defense for Policy to Deputy Assistant to the President for National Security, National Security Council, "Rwanda: Jamming Civilian Radio Broadcasts," May 5, 1994.

19. Smith, "Impact of Hate Media."

20. "Journalists Jailed for Inciting Rwandan Genocide," *The Guardian*, December 4, 2003.

21. "Statement by President Biden on Russia's Unprovoked and Unjustified Attack on Ukraine," The White House, February 23, 2022.

22. Rachel Oswald, "Lawmakers United in Outrage over Putin's 'Unprovoked' Invasion of Ukraine," Roll Call, February 24, 2022.

23. Ibid.

24. Bryce Greene, "Calling Russia's Attack 'Unprovoked' Lets US Off the Hook," Fairness & Accuracy in Reporting, March 4, 2022.

25. Greene, "Calling Russia's Attack 'Unprovoked.'"

26. Geoff Norman, "Critical Thinking and Critical Appraisal," in *International Handbook of Research in Medical Education*, eds. Geoff R. Norman, Cees P. M. van der Vleuten, David I. Newble, Diana H. J. M. Dolmans, Karen V. Mann, Arthur Rothman, and Lynn Curry (Boston: Kluwer Academic Publishers, 2002), 277–98.

27. M. Neil Browne and Stuart M. Keeley, *Asking the Right Questions: A Guide to Critical Thinking* (New York: Pearson, 2013).

28. Felix Kaufmann, "Truth and Logic." *Philosophy and Phenomenological Research* 1, no. 1 (1940): 59–69.

29. For more on primary, secondary, and tertiary sources, see Mark Brilliant, "Research & Writing Guide," Department of History, University of California Berkeley, accessed May 25, 2022.

30. For more on formal and informal logical fallacies, see "The Fallacy Files

Taxonomy of Logical Fallacies;" see also Jacob E. Van Vleet, *Informal Logical Fallacies: A Brief Guide*, Revised Edition (Lanham, MD: Hamilton Books, 2021).

31. Marios Pittalis and Constantinos Christou, "Types of Reasoning in 3d Geometry Thinking and Their Relation with Spatial Ability," *Educational Studies in Mathematics* 75, no. 2 (2010): 196.

32. Ibid.

33. Thorleif Lund, "A Metamodel of Central Inferences in Empirical Research," *Scandinavian Journal of Educational Research* 49, no. 4 (2005): 385–398.

34. Jennifer L. Eberhardt, *Biased: Uncovering the Hidden Prejudice That Shapes What We See, Think, and Do* (New York: Viking, 2018), 6–7.

35. Ziva Kunda, "The Case for Motivated Reasoning," *Psychological Bulletin* 108, no. 3 (1990): 480.

36. University at Buffalo, "How We Support Our False Beliefs," Science Daily, August 23, 2009.

37. Carl Sagan, *The Demon-Haunted World: Science as a Candle in the Dark* (New York: Random House, 1995), 12.

38. "Word of the Year 2016," Oxford Languages, accessed March 16, 2022.

39. Walter Lippmann, *Public Opinion* (New Brunswick, NJ, and London: Transaction Publishers, 1998[1922]), 98–99.

40. Stuart Hall, "The Whites of Their Eyes: Racist Ideologies and the Media," in *Gender, Race, and Class in Media*, eds. G. Dines and J. M. Humez (Thousand Oaks, CA: Sage, 1995), 18–22.

41. Kimberlé Crenshaw, "Mapping the Margins: Intersectionality, Identity Politics, and Violence against Women of Color," *Stanford Law Review* 43, no. 6 (1991): 1241–99.

42. Clark Merrefield, "How Early U.S. Newspapers Brokered Slavery," The Journalist's Resource, August 10, 2020.

43. Darnell Hunt and Ana-Christina Ramon, *Hollywood Diversity Report 2020* (Los Angeles: UCLA, 2020) 40–51.

44. Nicki Minaj, Twitter, September 13, 2021, 2:44pm.

45. "Tucker Carlson Uses Nicki Minaj's Tweet about Her Cousin's Friends Swollen Testicles to Raise Doubt about Effectiveness of Vaccine," Media Matters for America, September 13, 2021.

46. *Studio Responsibility Index* (GLAAD Media Institute, 2021), 12–15.

47. Hunt and Ramon, *Hollywood Diversity Report 2020*, 3–17.

48. Rosina Lippi-Green, "Teaching Children How to Discriminate: What We Learn from the Big Bad Wolf," in *English with an Accent* (Routledge, 2012).

49. *Where We Are on TV* (GLAAD Media Institute, 2021), 9–30.

50. Elana Shepert, "UBC Professor Becomes Massive TikTok Star with Hilarious Vaccine Literacy Videos: 'How Cool Is It That I Can Make a Vaccine in the Lab?'" Vancouver Is Awesome, March 8, 2021.

51. Ibid.

52. "Editorial Board: On Earth Day, Promote Greater Scientific Literacy," *Mercury News & East Bay Times,* April 22, 2021.

53. National Literacy Trust, "What is Literacy?," April 29, 2021.

54. Deborah Tannen, "The Medium Is the Metamessage: Conversational Style in New Media Interaction," *Discourse 2.0: Language and New Media,* 2013, 99–117.

55. Thomas Paterson and Lauren Hanley, "Political Warfare in the Digital Age: Cyber Subversion, Information Operations and 'Deep Fakes.'" *Australian Journal of International Affairs* 74, no. 4 (2020): 439–454. For more on "deep fakes," see Jennifer LaGarde and Darren Hudgins, "A Deep Dive into Deep Fakes: Media Literacy in a World Where Seeing Is No Longer Believing," *School Library Journal,* February 25, 2020.

56. Ben Parker, "How Advertisers Defund Crisis Journalism," The New Humanitarian, January 27, 2021.

57. Ibid.

58. Ibid.

59. Ibid.

60. Gianfranco Polizzi, "Information Literacy in the Digital Age: Why Critical Digital Literacy Matters for Democracy," in *Informed Societies: Why Information Literacy Matters for Citizenship, Participation and Democracy*, ed. Stéphane Goldstein (London: Facet Publishing, 2020), 1–24.

61. Pinar Akman, "We Can't Tackle Platform Competition Issues Without Increasing Digital Literacy," World Economic Forum, June 3, 2021.

62. Shoshana Zuboff, *The Age of Surveillance Capitalism: The Fight for the Future at the New Frontier of Power* (New York: Public Affairs, 2019).

63. Aaron Mak, "The Industry: How Facebook Made Those Eerie 'People You May Know' Suggestions," Slate, December 19, 2018.

64. Eli Pariser, *The Filter Bubble: How the New Personalized Web is Changing What We Read and How We Think,* (New York: Penguin, 2011).

65. Siva Vaidhyanathan, *Anti-Social Media: How Facebook Disconnects Us and Undermines Democracy* (New York: Oxford University Press, 2018)

66. See "About Us," Propwatch Project, accessed May 25, 2022, and "Propaganda Techniques: Fear, Uncertainty, and Doubt," Propwatch Project, accessed May 25, 2022.

67. Zuboff, *Age of Surveillance Capitalism*.

68. Ibid.

69. Bianca Bosker, "The Binge Breaker," *The Atlantic*, November 2016.

70. See, for example, Scott Jashik, "Do Algorithms Lead Admissions in the Wrong Direction?" Inside Higher Ed, September 27, 2021.

71. Alex Engler, "Enrollment Algorithms Are Contributing to the Crises of Higher Education," Brookings, September 14, 2021.

72. Ibid.

73. Carole Cadwalladr and Emma Graham-Harrison, "Revealed: 50 Million Facebook Profiles Harvested for Cambridge Analytica in Major Data Breach," *The Guardian*, March 17, 2018; and Matthew Rosenberg, Nicholas Confessore, and Carole Cadwalladr, "How Trump Consultants Exploited the Facebook Data of Millions," *New York Times*, March 17, 2018.

74. Rosenberg, Confessore, and Cadwalladr, "How Trump Consultants Exploited."

75. Alyssa Satara, "If You Don't Fully Understand the Cambridge Analytica Scandal, Read This Simplified Version," Inc., March 30, 2018.

76. Rosenberg, Confessore, and Cadwalladr, "How Trump Consultants Exploited."

77. Daniel Geschke, Jan Lorenz, and Peter Holtz, "The Triple-Filter Bubble: Using Agent-Based Modelling to Test a Meta-Theoretical Framework for the Emergence of Filter Bubbles and Echo Chambers," *British Journal of Social Psychology*, October 12, 2018.

78. Kate Klonick, "The New Governors: The People, Rules, and Processes Governing Online Speech," *Harvard Law Review* 131 (2018): 1598–1670, 1625.

79. Daniel Zhang, Saurabh Mishra, Erik Brynjolfsson, John Etchemendy, Deep Ganguli, Barbara Grosz, Terah Lyons, James Manyika, Juan Carlos Niebles, Michael Sellitto, Yoav Shoham, Jack Clark, and Raymond Perrault, "The AI Index 2021 Annual Report," AI Index Steering Committee, Human-Centered AI Institute, Stanford University, Stanford, CA, March 2021.

80. avram anderson and Andy Lee Roth, "Queer Erasure: Internet Browsing Can

Be Biased against LGBTQ People, New Exclusive Research Shows," *Index on Censorship* 49, no. 1 (Winter 2021): 75–77.

81. Shakira Smith, Oliver L Haimson, Claire Fitzsimmons, and Nikki Echarte Brown, "Censorship of Marginalized Communities on Instagram," Salty Algorithmic Bias Collective, September 2021.

82. Safiya Umoja Noble, *Algorithms of Oppression: How Search Engines Reinforce Racism* (New York: New York University Press, 2018), 24.

83. Virginia Eubanks, *Automating Inequality: How High-Tech Tools Profile, Police, and Punish the Poor* (New York: St. Martin's Press, 2017).

84. Noble, *Algorithms of Oppression*, 1.

85. Noble, *Algorithms of Oppression*, 1.

86. See, for example, Andy Lee Roth, "The New Gatekeepers: How Proprietary Algorithms Increasingly Determine the News We See," The Markaz Review, March 15, 2021.

87. "Building the Foundations for a Decentralized Virtual World," Decentraland, February 19, 2020.

88. "Thanos Is Coming! Get Him First in the Thanos Cup," Fortnite (Epic Games), June 18, 2021; Fortnite, Twitter, April 23, 2020, 8:21p.m.

89. Elizabeth Howcroft, "Virtual Real Estate Plot Sells for Record $2.4 Million," Reuters, November 23, 2021.

90. Marc Goodman, *Future Crimes: Everything Is Connected, Everyone Is Vulnerable, and What We Can Do about It*, (New York: Doubleday, 2015).

91. Brian Stelter, "Google Unveils Plans to Boost News Subscriptions and Combat Fake News," CNN Business, March 20, 2018.

92. Dallas W. Smythe, "Communications: Blindspot of Western Marxism," *Canadian Journal of Political and Social Theory* 1, no. 3 (1977).

93. Brad Adgate, "Ad Agency Forecast: Expect the Advertising Market to Rebound in 2021," *Forbes*, December 14, 2020.

94. Pamela McClintock, "2019 Global Box Office Revenue Hit Record $42.5B Despite 4 Percent Dip in U.S.," *Hollywood Reporter*, January 10, 2020; Kevin Anderton, "The Business of Video Games: Market Share for Gaming Platforms in 2019," *Forbes*, June 26, 2019; Cally Russell, "Adidas or Nike? Which Retail Giant Is Winning the Sneakers War?," *Forbes*, August 22, 2019.

95. "Manufacturing Consumers," *The Ad and the Ego*, dir. Harold Boihem (Burbank, CA: Parallax Pictures, 1997).

96. "Understanding the Language of Persuasion," Action Coalition for Media

Education, accessed May 25, 2022.

97. Sut Jhally, *Killing Us Softly 4* (Northampton, MA: Media Education Foundation, 2010).

98. Thomas Alsop, "Apple's Market Share of PC Unit Shipments in the United States from 2013 to 2022, by Quarter," Statistia, April 13, 2022.

99. William James, *Principles of Psychology* (New York: Henry Holt and Company, 1890), 403–4.

100. Tim Wu, "Blind Spot: The Attention Economy and the Law," Columbia Law School Scholarship Archive, 2019.

101. See, for example, Siva Vaidhyanathan, *Anti-Social Media: How Facebook Disconnects Us and Undermines Democracy* (New York: Oxford University Press, 2018), and Tim Wu, *The Attention Merchants: The Epic Scramble to Get Inside Our Heads* (New York: Vintage Books, 2017).

102. Wu, "Blind Spot."

103. Ibid.

104. Stefano DellaVigna and Eliana La Ferrara, "Economic and Social Impacts of the Media," in *Handbook of Media Economics*, eds. Simon Anderson, Joel Waldfogel, and David Strömberg (New York: Elsevier, 2015), 723–768.

105. Kermit Pattison, "Worker, Interrupted: The Cost of Task Switching," Fast Company, July 28, 2008.

106. Wu, *The Attention Merchants*, 125.

107. For more ideas, check out the annual Screen-Free Week.

108. "Home," Adbusters, accessed March 17, 2021.

109. Marc Steiner, interview with Chris Hedges, "War Profiteers Are Fueling This Crisis," The Real News Network, March 4, 2022.

110. Ibid.

111. Chris Hedges, *War Is a Force That Gives Us Meaning* (New York: Public Affairs, 2002).

112. Larry Buchanan, Quoctrung Bui, and Jugal K. Patel, "Black Lives Matter May Be the Largest Movement in U.S. History," *New York Times,* July 3, 2020.

113. Ibid.

114. Rich Buhler and Staff, "Six Corporations Own 90 Percent of News Media—Truth!" Truth or Fiction, March 17, 2015; Ashley Lutz, "These 6 Corporations Control 90% of the Media In America," *Business Insider*, June 14, 2012.

115. Edward Herman and Noam Chomsky, *Manufacturing Consent: The Political*

Economy of the Mass Media, (New York, New York: Pantheon Books, 1988).

116. Steve Macek and Andy Lee Roth, "It's True That Corporate Media Is Biased—But Not in the Ways Right-Wingers Say," Truthout, November 27, 2020.

117. On news slant, see, for example, Robert M. Entman, "Framing Bias: Media in the Distribution of Power," *Journal of Communication* 57 (2007): 163-73.

118. Thomas Moore, "TV News Ratings, Online Readership Plunge during Biden's First 100 Days," The Hill, April 30, 2021.

119. "What Is Modern Censorship?" Project Censored, accessed May 25, 2022.

120. For more on the types of important news stories that corporate news media either marginalize or blockade, see Project Censored's *State of the Free Press 2022*, edited by Andy Lee Roth and Mickey Huff (Fair Oaks, CA and New York: The Censored Press and Seven Stories Press, 2022), 23-28.

121. Jennifer Allen, Baird Howland, Markus Mobius, David Rothschild, and Duncan J. Watts, "Evaluating the Fake News Problem at the Scale of the Information Ecosystem," *Science Advances* 6, no. 14, (April 3, 2020).

122. Nolan Higdon, *The Anatomy of Fake News: A Critical News Literacy Education*, (Oakland, California: University of California Press, 2020), 3.

123. John Christie, "Anonymous Sources: Leaving Journalism's False God Behind," Poynter, April 23, 2014.

124. Steve Macek and Andy Lee Roth, "Corporate Media Largely Ignore Labor Issues. Let's Make Them Visible," Truthout, January 17, 2022.

125. See, for example, Nolan Higdon and Mickey Huff, *Let's Agree to Disagree: A Critical Thinking Guide to Communication, Conflict Management, and Critical Media Literacy* (New York and London: Routledge, 2022).

126. Daniel C. Dennett, *Intuition Pumps and Other Tools for Thinking* (New York: W. W. Norton & Company, 2013).

127. See, for example, M. Neil Browne and Stuart M. Keeley, *Asking the Right Questions: A Guide to Critical Thinking*, Twelfth Edition (New York: Pearson, 2018).

128. "How to Write a Lead," Purdue Online Writing Lab, accessed May 25, 2022.

129. Hari Sreenivasan, interview with Ainissa Ramirez, "Twitter and the Telegraph," SciTech Now (PBS), season 5, episode 12, January 14, 2019.

130. Newseum's searchable "Today's Front Pages."

Index

Index